# DORLING KINDERSLEY DK EYEWITNESS BOOKS

# ARMS & ARMOR

Silver-hilted
robe sword,
c. 1710

Flintlock pocket
pistol, c. 1770

Rapier, c. 1625

Silver-hilted
hunting sword,
c. 1750

Flintlock
"Tower" pistol,
c.1800

Pepperbox revolver,
c. 1855

Medieval dagger, c. 1400

Gauntlet, c. 1580

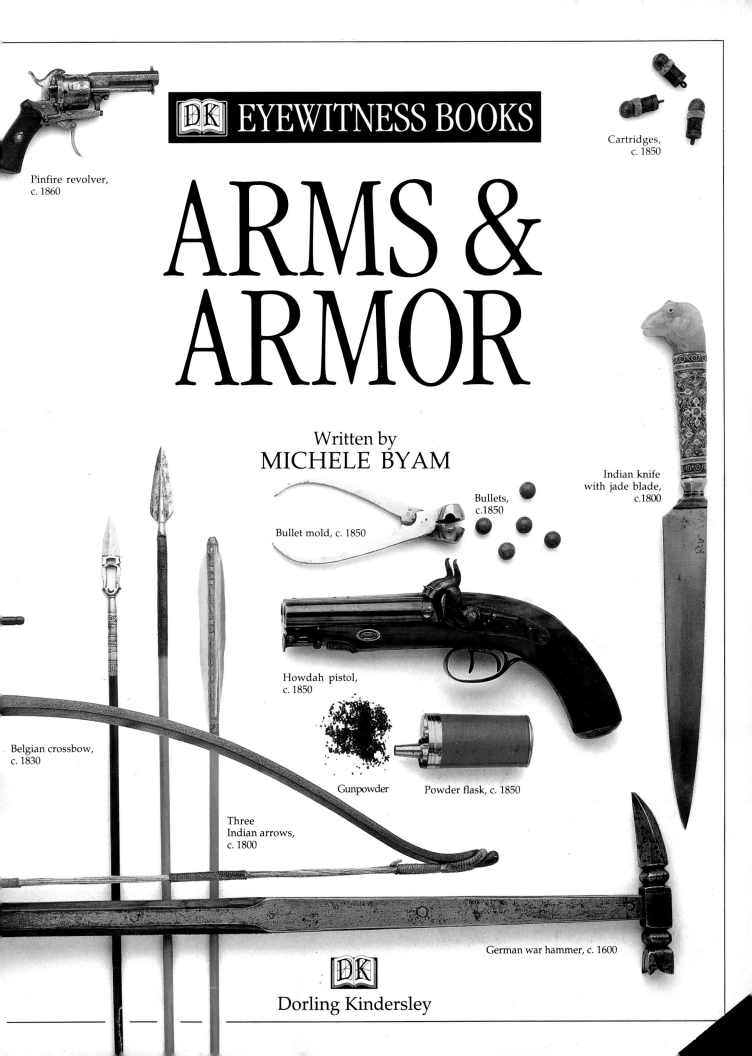

# DK EYEWITNESS BOOKS

# ARMS & ARMOR

Written by
## MICHELE BYAM

Pinfire revolver,
c. 1860

Cartridges,
c. 1850

Bullet mold, c. 1850

Bullets,
c.1850

Indian knife
with jade blade,
c.1800

Howdah pistol,
c. 1850

Belgian crossbow,
c. 1830

Three
Indian arrows,
c. 1800

Gunpowder

Powder flask, c. 1850

German war hammer, c. 1600

## DK
Dorling Kindersley

Niam Niam, a ceremonial
knife from Sudan, Africa

Maratha "crow-bill" war
pick from northern India

## Dorling Kindersley

LONDON, NEW YORK, AUCKLAND, DELHI, JOHANNESBURG,
MUNICH, PARIS and SYDNEY

### For a full catalog, visit

DK www.dk.com

**Project editor** Michele Byam
**Managing art editor** Jane Owen
**Special photography** Dave King
**Editorial consultants** David Harding

This Eyewitness ® Book has been conceived by
Dorling Kindersley Limited and Editions Gallimard

© 1988 Dorling Kindersley Limited
This edition © 2000 Dorling Kindersley Limited
First American edition, 1988

Published in the United States by
Dorling Kindersley Publishing, Inc.
95 Madison Avenue
New York, NY 10016
2 4 6 8 10 9 7 5 3 1

Dorling Kindersley books are available at special discounts for bulk
purchases for sales promotions or premiums. Special editions, including
personalized covers, excerpts of existing guides, and corporate imprints
can be created in large quantities for specific needs. For more information,
contact Special Markets Dept., Dorling Kindersley Publishing, Inc., 95
Madison Ave., New York, NY 10016; Fax: (800) 600-9098

Library of Congress Cataloging-in-Publication Data
Byam, Michele.
Arms & Armor / written by Michele Byam.
(Eyewitness books)
Includes index.
Summary: A photo essay examining the design, construction, and
uses of hand weapons and armor from a Stone Age axe to the
revolvers and rifles of the Wild West. 1. Arms and armor — Juvenile
literature. [1. Arms and armor] I. King, Dave, ill.
II. Title. III. Title: Arms and armor. IV. Series.
UB800.B93 2000 355.8'241 87-26449
ISBN 0-7894-5837-3 (pb)
ISBN 0-7894-5836-5 (hc)

Color reproduction by Colourscan, Singapore
Printed in China by Toppan Printing Co. (Shenzhen) Ltd.

Copper dagger of
the Kasai people of
West Africa

Chinese sword in
wooden sheath,
clad in tortoiseshell
with brass mounts

# Contents

Spiked iron
bracelet
from eastern
Sudan, Africa

Buffalo horn
knuckleduster
from southern India

Tiger claw
from northern India

# Prehistoric weapons

IN ORDER TO HUNT, attack others, or defend themselves, people have always used weapons. In the Early Palaeolithic or Old Stone Age, the tiny, scattered communities used weapons mainly for hunting. Early people discovered that if they chipped hard stones such as flint into a pointed shape, the stones could be used for killing and skinning animals.

Thousands of years later, in the Upper Palaeolithic or Later Stone Age, weapons were changed radically by the invention of the handle or haft. By lashing a handle onto an axe head, or spearhead, prehistoric people found that their hunting and attacking weapons became both stronger and more reliable.

Flint flakes

The illustration (above) shows how hand axes were probably held

**FLINT NODULE** *above*
The first tools and weapons would have come from a nodule (lump) of flint rock like this. To fashion a hand axe, stone flakes were broken off with another stone.

**BREAKING OFF A FLINT FLAKE**
The first stage of preparing a flint tool or weapon was to break off a large flint flake with a stone hammer.

**STRIKING OFF CHIPS**
After the stone hammer had made a rough shape, the remaining core was fashioned into a tool or weapon with a wooden or bone hammer.

**PRESSURE FLAKING**
A more refined method of working a weapon or tool to a desired shape was by using a bone, stone, or wooden object to pare or shave the flint's surface.

**CRUDE PALAEOLITHIC HAND AXE,**
**250,000-70,000 B.C.** *right*
Although made during the same period in pre-history as the axe above right, this weapon or tool is not as well crafted.

**TWO PALAEOLITHIC HAND AXES,**
**c. 300,000 - 200,000 B.C.**
These axes or chopping tools, made by an ancestor of modern man known as *Homo erectus*, are hardly recognizable as tools or weapons.

*Held at wide end*

**DEER HUNTING**
An old engraving shows a New Stone Age hunter killing a deer with a flint axe fastened to a wooden handle.

**TWO SHAPED PALAEOLITHIC HAND AXES,**
c. 250,000-70,000 B.C. *left and below*
Hand axes were certainly used by
Palaeolithic people as weapons
when hunting animals, but it is
purely guesswork whether an axe
like this was ever used as a
battle-axe in warfare.

*Rough
cutting edge*

**MIDDLE PALAEOLITHIC
HAND AXES,**
c. 80,000-40,000 B.C. *right*
Of a similar date, these
two hand axes were
made by a type of early
people known as
Neanderthal man.

A cave painting of archers,
painted between 12,000 and 3,000
B.C., found at Cueva Remigia,
Spain (above)

*Spearhead tip*

**SPEARHEAD, c. 20,000 B.C.**
By the time this possible
spearhead was made by
*Homo sapiens sapiens* or
modern man, handles
had been invented,
which radically
changed weapons
and tools.

**STONE AGE MAMMOTH HUNT**
Hunters in the Old Stone Age needed both bravery
and cleverness to trap and kill large animals. Having
been driven into a pit, this woolly mammoth, an
extinct type of elephant, is being battered to
death with rocks. The spears sticking into the
mammoth's sides would have been
made of sharpened wood.

**STONE AGE
HUNTERS**
Cave paintings
found in European
countries such as
Spain and France
show either hunters
or the animals
they killed.

# Missile weapons

ANYONE WHO HAS EVER thrown a stick or a stone, fired a catapult, or shot an arrow from a bow has used a missile weapon. Indeed, such weapons have been used for both hunting and fighting since prehistoric times. More unusual missile weapons include the boomerang, traditional weapon of the native Australian aborigine, and the curiously shaped throwing weapons used by the tribespeople of Central and West Africa. The simplicity of these weapons is deceptive, for when used by skilled throwers they are just as effective as more complex hand weapons.

**Stone arrowhead**

**ASSYRIAN HORSEMAN**
In this 7th century B.C. relief, an Assyrian carries a lance, a sword and a bow with arrows.

**Flatter on one side than the other**

**FIGHTING BOOMERANG** *left*
The large wooden boomerangs used by aborigines in war are designed to fly straight and do not return to their throwers even if they miss their targets.

**Flat piece of hard wood**

**Grip**

**Striking edge**

**THROWING A BOOMERANG**
When used by a skilled thrower, such as this Australian aborigine, a boomerang can be sent great distances.

**PARRYING STICK** *above*
Sticks are defensive rather than offensive weapons. This aborigine parrying stick deflects missile weapons such as spears and boomerangs.

**Club's pointed end**

**THROWING CLUB** *above right*
An aborigine aiming this wooden throwing club would try to stun his victim with the weapon's pointed end. Some of the wooden war clubs used by Pacific Islanders and African tribesmen are also used as missile weapons.

**ABORIGINES HUNTING**
Australian aborigines are peaceful people who rarely use their weapons for fighting. In this 19th-century painting a group of aborigines are hunting game with hand clubs, shields, and multi-tipped fishing spears.

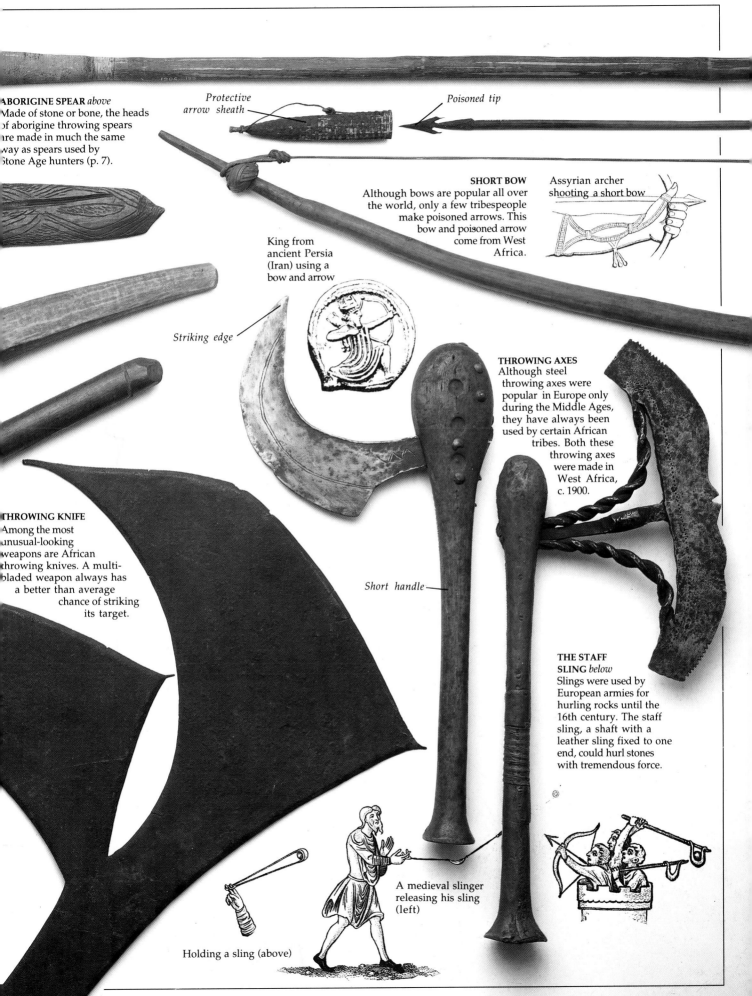

**ABORIGINE SPEAR** *above*
Made of stone or bone, the heads of aborigine throwing spears are made in much the same way as spears used by Stone Age hunters (p. 7).

*Protective arrow sheath*

*Poisoned tip*

**SHORT BOW**
Although bows are popular all over the world, only a few tribespeople make poisoned arrows. This bow and poisoned arrow come from West Africa.

Assyrian archer shooting a short bow

King from ancient Persia (Iran) using a bow and arrow

*Striking edge*

**THROWING AXES**
Although steel throwing axes were popular in Europe only during the Middle Ages, they have always been used by certain African tribes. Both these throwing axes were made in West Africa, c. 1900.

**THROWING KNIFE**
Among the most unusual-looking weapons are African throwing knives. A multi-bladed weapon always has a better than average chance of striking its target.

*Short handle*

**THE STAFF SLING** *below*
Slings were used by European armies for hurling rocks until the 16th century. The staff sling, a shaft with a leather sling fixed to one end, could hurl stones with tremendous force.

A medieval slinger releasing his sling (left)

Holding a sling (above)

9

# The first warriors

THE DISCOVERY OF METALS such as copper and bronze, first used in south west Europe about six thousand years ago, changed forever the making of both tools and weapons. In the early part of the Bronze Age, axes and spears were still "tanged" - bound to a handle or haft by leather strips or string. By the end of the Bronze Age, weapons were more firmly secured to handles by sockets. In the 6th and 5th centuries B.C., Celtic tribesmen in Europe began to make tools and weapons from iron as well as bronze. The richly ornamental culture that the migrating Celts spread across Europe at the beginning of the Iron Age is well-illustrated by their finely crafted weapons.

A fragment of copper or bronze, used for making weapons or tools

*Socket for insertion of haft (handle)*

*Loop through which a cord tied axehead to haft*

**THREE BRONZE AXE HEADS, c. 750-650 B.C.**
By the Late European Bronze Age, bronzesmiths had learned to make socketed axes into which wooden handles were inserted. Axes were used for warfare or woodworking.

Three flint arrowheads

*Tang*

*Barb*

**HALBERD BLADE, c. 2300-1600 B.C.** *below*
Made either in Ireland or on the European mainland, this copper halberd, could be used for either cutting or chopping, making it useful as both a battle-axe and a spear.

**FLINT ARROWHEADS, c. 2700-1800 B.C.** *above*
Bows and arrows were used for the first time during the Mesolithic Age (Middle Stone Age). About 2500 B.C. these "barbed and tanged" arrowheads were used for hunting or warfare.

Celtic warrior, c. 450 B.C., carrying a sword and spear

**BRONZE SPEARHEAD, c. 900-800 B.C.** *above*
Crude spears were first used in the New Stone Age (pp. 6-7). By the Bronze Age, spearheads like this were made by skilled bronzesmiths.

**BRONZE SWORD POMMELS AND HILTS**
The fine engraving on these swords shows the craftsmanship of Late Bronze Age bronzesmiths. Weapons like these would have belonged to chieftains.

*Grip would have had wood, bone, or horn plates, riveted on either side and wrapped with leather*

**BRONZE AGE SWORD, c. 900-800 B.C.**
This gracefully shaped Late Bronze Age sword was designed as a slashing weapon.

*Double-edged blade*

*Long wooden handle*

## BRONZE AGE HELMET, c. 15th CENTURY B.C.
Found in East Germany, this Bronze Age warrior's helmet would originally have had protective earpieces.

19th-century engraving of a Celtic chieftain carrying a heavy spear

## BRONZE HELMET, c. 1st CENTURY A.D.
This horned Iron Age warrior's helmet was found in the river Thames in London. It was almost certainly a parade helmet, as it was not sturdy enough to wear in battle.

## IRON AGE SHIELD, c. 200-100 B.C. *left*
Recovered from the river Thames, this beautifully decorated shield was probably for ceremonial use rather than warfare. The bronze sheet originally had a wood backing, and the shield's inserts are colored glass studs.

## "VERCINGETORIX BEFORE CAESAR" *right*
The leader of the Gauls in their revolt against Roman rule, Vercingetorix was captured by Julius Caesar in 52 B.C. In this painting, the Celtic weapons on the ground include a shield, helmet, and sword.

*Dagger tip*

## IRON AGE DAGGER IN SHEATH , c. 550 B.C.
This early British iron dagger would have belonged to a tribal chief. The bronze sheath would have hung from his belt by iron loops.

*Guard*

*Wood lining wrapped with bronze strips*

## EARLY BRONZE AGE DAGGERS
Central European tribesmen used these daggers for fighting at close quarters.

*Double-edged blade*

# A Roman legionary

THE TWO GREATEST ARMIES of ancient times were the Macedonian army under Alexander the Great and the Roman army. From 334 to 326 B.C, Macedonia, a small Greek state, had a superb army built around the phalanx - solid lines of spear-carrying infantry. The basis of the Roman army was the legion - units of infantry with supporting cavalry. Between 800 B.C. and A.D. 200 it was the Roman army's continuing response to enemy weapons and to changes in available materials, together with good discipline and organization, that brought Rome to its preeminent position as ruler of the ancient world. The armor and weapons shown on these pages are accurate replicas of equipment carried by the Roman legions.

A Roman standard-bearer wearing a *gladius*

## A Greek hoplite

A Greek foot soldier or hoplite's equipment included a metal helmet, a leather or mail breastplate, a metal shield, and leg armor. He carried a thrusting spear and a short sword.

**GREEK VASE**
Much of our knowledge of ancient Greek arms and armor comes from decorations on vases of the time. Here, the Greek hero Achilles is shown killing Penthesilea. Painted about 540 B.C., the two figures depicted give a good idea of the helmet styles and body armor of the period.

Gladius *handle made of wood or bone*

**MILITARY DAGGER**
Soldiers carried a short dagger called a *pugio* on the belt at their left hip. Its iron scabbard was often decorated with inlaid enamel patterns. Roman works of art only depict soldiers wearing a *pugio* in the lst centuries B.C. to A.D., which suggests that it was not considered an essential weapon.

*Grip made of bronze*

**INFANTRY SWORD**
The *gladius* was a short, double-edged sword that was used more for thrusting than for cutting. It was worn by infantrymen at the right hip either on a belt or a baldric (shoulder belt). The scabbard was sometimes highly decorated, as in this example from the 1st century A.D.

**CORINTHIAN HELMET**
The Corinthian-type Greek helmet, first made in the 8th century B.C., reached the elegant shape shown here in the 7th century B.C. Only the eyes and mouth were uncovered, providing almost complete protection. When not fighting, the soldier often wore his helmet on top of his head for comfort.

*Double-edged blade*

*Scabbard made of wood covered in leather and decorated in bronze*

Iron scabbard with loops for attachment to belt

**SCENE FROM THE ILIAD**
A 19th-century picture of soldiers from the Greek epic poem the *Iliad*. Said to have been written in the 8th century B.C. by Homer, the poem tells of events in the final year of the mythological Trojan War. The warriors are in fact wearing Roman-style bronze breastplates and helmets.

Horsehair crest

Holder for horsehair crest

**IRON HELMET**
The iron Imperial Gallic helmet (c.A.D. 30) had a deep neck guard, a brow guard to deflect sword strokes, and ear guards of doubtful value.

**BRONZE HELMET**
This bronze helmet (c.50 B.C.) is a very simple design that carried a horsehair crest. Later helmets of this type had feathered crests.

*Broad cheekpieces hinged to side of helmet and tied under chin with straps or cords*

**THROWING SPEARS** *left*
The head of the *hasta* (right) is a familiar shape for a spear, but the long head of the *pilum* (left) was designed to pierce a shield and then continue on into the soldier behind it.

Long iron point

**ROMAN GLADIATORS**
Although their style was flashier than that of the Roman army, gladiators often led the way in new weapon designs such as lighter rectangular shields.

Victorian depiction of Roman legionaries

*Armor laced together at the front and upper part of armor hooked to lower part by bronze hooks*

**BODY ARMOR**
Made of iron strips, the *lorica segmentata*, an early cuirass (p. 26), was worn from early in the 1st century A.D. until the 3rd century. It partially replaced the earlier chain mail and scale armor. The strips were held together by leather straps on the inside, and the armor had many bronze fittings.

*Long haft made of ash*

# Weapons from the Dark Ages

THE DARK AGES WAS THE PERIOD in European history between the 400s and 900s when Germanic and Scandinavian tribesmen - Saxons and Norsemen (Vikings ) - raided and settled in Belgium, the Netherlands, England, France, and Spain. Our knowledge of this period comes not only from surviving weapons and equipment, but from textiles such as the Bayeux tapestry, woven to celebrate the invasion of England in 1066 by the Normans (Norsemen) of north west France.

*Flat pommel*

**ANGLO-SAXON SWORD, c. 500-600** *above*
Swords were used only by Saxons of high rank, such as the king (above), shown with his shield bearer. He is wearing a chain-mail shirt.

*Missing grip would have been made of wood and possibly covered with leather, bone, or horn*

**VIKING SWORD BLADE** *above*
Made by skilled craftsmen, Viking sword blades were double edged with slightly blunted tips.

*Original shaft probably made of ash*

**SHORT SPEAR, c. 400-500** *above*
Short-headed Saxon spears were used for both stabbing and throwing.

*Iron head*

**LONG SPEAR, c. 400-500** *above*
Long-headed Saxon spears were used by or against cavalry.

**VIKING GOD**
Tyr, the god of war, was believed to give victory in battle, so Viking swords were often marked with the letter T.

**ANGLO-SAXON HELMET, c. 600**
Although recovered from a Saxon burial ground, this helmet resembles those worn by the Vikings.

## THE NORMANS ATTACK THE ENGLISH

A valuable document on the weapons of the Norman period, the Bayeux tapestry is a strip of embroidered linen that chronicles the Norman invasion of England in 1066.

*Inlaid pattern*

## SWORD GUARD, c. 1040

Made of metal, ivory, bone or horn, sword guards were often inlaid with precious metals.

*Rounded point*

*Shallow fuller (groove) lightens weight of blade*

*Curved cross-guard*

*Trilobed pommel*

## VIKING SWORD, c. 900-1000 *below*

A Viking's favorite weapon was his sword. Used for slashing rather than thrusting at an enemy, swords were carried in decorated scabbards.

*Grips, made of metal, horn, wood, or bone, were sometimes covered in leather*

## VIKING AXE, c. 900-1000

A Viking warrior swung his battle-axe around his head in an arc before landing an almost certainly fatal blow on an enemy or his horse.

## NORMAN ARCHER *right*

This detail from the Bayeux tapestry (above) shows an archer with his bow and arrows. He is wearing a typical Norman mail shirt and one-piece metal helmet.

*Norman knights using spurs and stirrups*

## NORMAN SPUR, c. 11th CENTURY

First used in ancient Greece and Rome, spurs helped the Norman knight, a skillful horseman, to control his horse in battle.

*Long handle for holding with two hands*

*Broad, crescent-shaped blade*

*Cutting edge made of hardened steel*

*Three Norman arrows (above and below)*

*Arrowhead made of iron*

## THE DISCOVERY OF GREENLAND

Explorers as well as warriors and traders, the Vikings, led by Eric the Red, discovered and colonized Greenland in c. 982.

*Sharply pointed Norman lance*

# European swords

O NE OF HUMANKIND'S oldest weapons, a sword consists of a hilt and a blade: the hilt has a pommel for balancing the weapon, a grip for holding it, and a guard for protecting the hand. The blade can be straight or curved and, according to whether the sword is designed for cutting, thrusting, or both, is either single or double edged and has a rounded or pointed tip. For centuries, swords were used mainly for cutting and were easy to hold with one hand. But by the 1400s, massive two-handed swords were in use - weapons so heavy that only the strongest soldiers could wield them.

*A 17th-century allegory of a sword-smith*

*Sword painted black to keep metal from rusting*

*Double-edged blade for thrusting through plate armor*

*Weight 15 lbs (7 kilos), length 5 ft (1.5 m)*

*Guard*

*Long, broad, double-edged blade*

**THE STORY OF KING ARTHUR**
There are many versions of the legends surrounding the partly mythical, partly historical figure of King Arthur. This illustration, by the Victorian artist Walter Crane, shows Arthur being saved from death by Sir Launcelot, who is carrying a typical medieval sword.

*Sharp point for thrusting*

The action of a single-edged cutting sword such as a saber

*Iron hilt with missing grip*

*Pommel representing a boar's head*

**CUTTING SWORD, c. 1580** *below*
With its slightly curved, single-edged and pointed blad this hunting sword or hanger best suited to a cutting action. Hangers were also worn by foo soldiers as military sidearms.

*Fuller or groove*

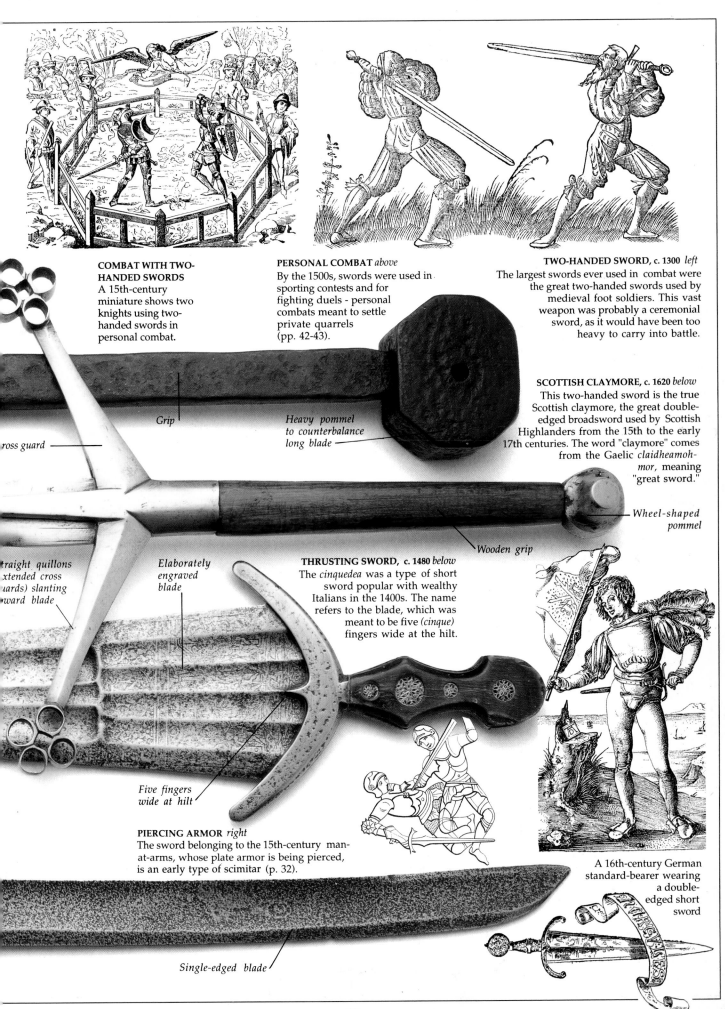

**COMBAT WITH TWO-HANDED SWORDS**
A 15th-century miniature shows two knights using two-handed swords in personal combat.

**PERSONAL COMBAT** *above*
By the 1500s, swords were used in sporting contests and for fighting duels - personal combats meant to settle private quarrels (pp. 42-43).

**TWO-HANDED SWORD, c. 1300** *left*
The largest swords ever used in combat were the great two-handed swords used by medieval foot soldiers. This vast weapon was probably a ceremonial sword, as it would have been too heavy to carry into battle.

**SCOTTISH CLAYMORE, c. 1620** *below*
This two-handed sword is the true Scottish claymore, the great double-edged broadsword used by Scottish Highlanders from the 15th to the early 17th centuries. The word "claymore" comes from the Gaelic *claidheamohmor*, meaning "great sword."

*Grip*

*Heavy pommel to counterbalance long blade*

*ross guard*

*Wheel-shaped pommel*

*Wooden grip*

*raight quillons xtended cross uards) slanting ward blade*

*Elaborately engraved blade*

**THRUSTING SWORD, c. 1480** *below*
The *cinquedea* was a type of short sword popular with wealthy Italians in the 1400s. The name refers to the blade, which was meant to be five (*cinque*) fingers wide at the hilt.

*Five fingers wide at hilt*

**PIERCING ARMOR** *right*
The sword belonging to the 15th-century man-at-arms, whose plate armor is being pierced, is an early type of scimitar (p. 32).

A 16th-century German standard-bearer wearing a double-edged short sword

*Single-edged blade*

17

# Crossbow versus longbow

DURING THE MIDDLE AGES the use of the bow in both hunting and battle was revolutionized by the appearance of the longbow and the crossbow. By combining archery with simple machinery, the crossbow proved a more deadly and accurate weapon than the ordinary bow (p. 9). Indeed some crossbows were so powerfully made they had to be loaded by a variety of mechanical devices. But despite the crossbow's greater range, it had a slower rate of fire than the longbow and was more expensive to make. The longbow was a much improved version of the ordinary bow and at a range of 100 yds (91 m) its steel-tipped arrows were deadly. With neither weapon having a clear lead over the other, many medieval armies contained corps of both longbowmen and crossbowmen.

Medieval iron arrowheads

Longbowmen, from a 15th-century manuscript

**SOLDIER USING CRANEQUIN**
The cranequin, a rack-and-pinion spanning device, first appeared in the 14th century. Its slow winding action made it more practical for hunting than battle.

## Firing a crossbow

1 Bowstring held in spanned (loaded) position by a rotating catch (the nut) set in crossbow tiller.
2 Bolt laid in groove along the top of stock and aimed by pressing rear of stock to cheek.
3 Bolt then released by pressing up the rear end of the trigger.

**ARCHERS DEFENDING A CITY** *left*
During the 15th century many fortified towns trained archers to defend the city to which they belonged. Note the crossbowman winding a cranequin (see above).

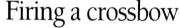

*Target arrowhead for contest*

## ENGLISH LONGBOW, c. 19th century

**ENGLISH YEW LONGBOW**
Constructed from a single piece of wood, usually yew, the longbow was a formidable weapon when fired by highly trained archers. Longbow lengths varied from country to country. In England the bow was usually the width of an archer's span between his outstretched arms, which in a tall man would equal his height.

*Horn nock or groove for attaching bowstring*

**Hook for attaching to bowstring**

### SPANNING LEVER
The goat's-foot lever was a tool used for spanning small crossbows. The limbs slid over pivots on either side of the bow's stock and the handle was then pulled back.

*Lever handle*

*Curved limbs for sliding over stock*

### ROBIN HOOD
The legendary English outlaw Robin Hood has always been associated with the longbow. Many of the ballads recounting his deeds tell of his skill as an archer.

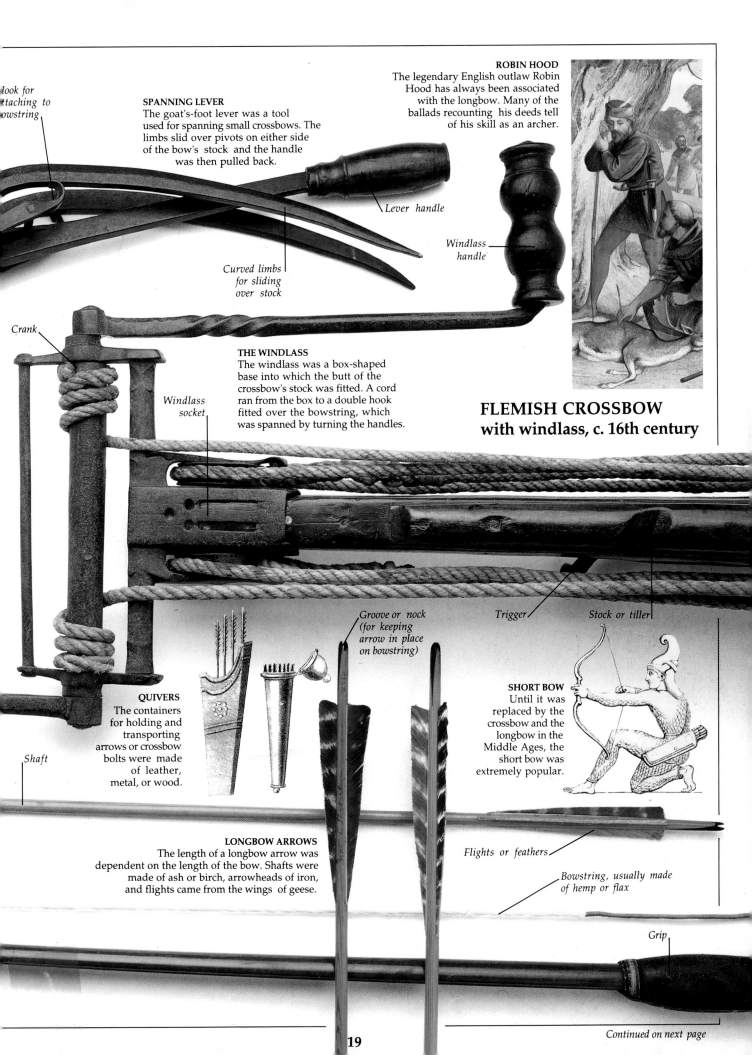

*Windlass handle*

*Crank*

### THE WINDLASS
The windlass was a box-shaped base into which the butt of the crossbow's stock was fitted. A cord ran from the box to a double hook fitted over the bowstring, which was spanned by turning the handles.

*Windlass socket*

## FLEMISH CROSSBOW
## with windlass, c. 16th century

*Groove or nock (for keeping arrow in place on bowstring)*

*Trigger*

*Stock or tiller*

### QUIVERS
The containers for holding and transporting arrows or crossbow bolts were made of leather, metal, or wood.

### SHORT BOW
Until it was replaced by the crossbow and the longbow in the Middle Ages, the short bow was extremely popular.

*Shaft*

### LONGBOW ARROWS
The length of a longbow arrow was dependent on the length of the bow. Shafts were made of ash or birch, arrowheads of iron, and flights came from the wings of geese.

*Flights or feathers*

*Bowstring, usually made of hemp or flax*

*Grip*

**19**

*Continued on next page*

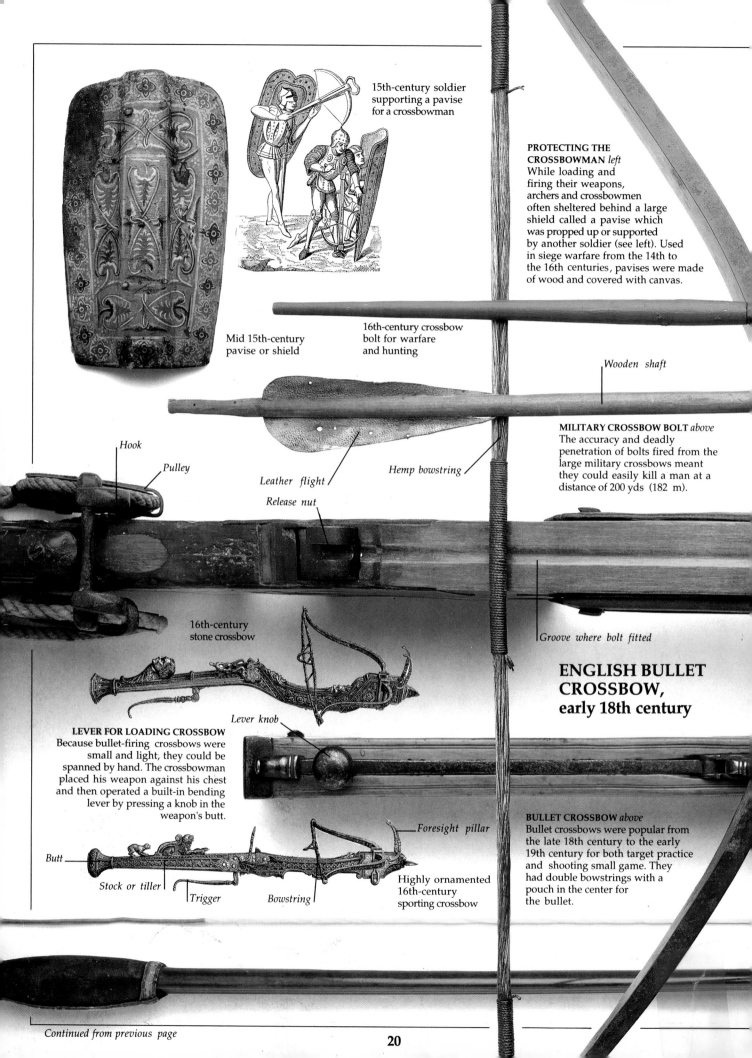

15th-century soldier supporting a pavise for a crossbowman

**PROTECTING THE CROSSBOWMAN** *left*
While loading and firing their weapons, archers and crossbowmen often sheltered behind a large shield called a pavise which was propped up or supported by another soldier (see left). Used in siege warfare from the 14th to the 16th centuries, pavises were made of wood and covered with canvas.

Mid 15th-century pavise or shield

16th-century crossbow bolt for warfare and hunting

*Wooden shaft*

**MILITARY CROSSBOW BOLT** *above*
The accuracy and deadly penetration of bolts fired from the large military crossbows meant they could easily kill a man at a distance of 200 yds (182 m).

*Hook*

*Pulley*

*Leather flight*

*Release nut*

*Hemp bowstring*

*Groove where bolt fitted*

16th-century stone crossbow

**ENGLISH BULLET CROSSBOW, early 18th century**

**LEVER FOR LOADING CROSSBOW**
Because bullet-firing crossbows were small and light, they could be spanned by hand. The crossbowman placed his weapon against his chest and then operated a built-in bending lever by pressing a knob in the weapon's butt.

*Lever knob*

*Butt*

*Stock or tiller*

*Trigger*

*Bowstring*

*Foresight pillar*

Highly ornamented 16th-century sporting crossbow

**BULLET CROSSBOW** *above*
Bullet crossbows were popular from the late 18th century to the early 19th century for both target practice and shooting small game. They had double bowstrings with a pouch in the center for the bullet.

*Continued from previous page*

A group of 15th-century
French crossbowmen
shooting from
behind
pavises

**WILLIAM TELL**
According to legend, the
national hero of
Switzerland, William Tell,
was forced to shoot an apple
from the head of his own
son with a crossbow.
Tell was being punished
for refusing to swear
allegiance to the
Austrians, who
ruled his country
in the 1300s.

Iron bolt
heads

Two 16th-century
military bolts

Steel tip

**INCENDIARY (FLAMING) ARROWS**
Incendiary arrows and bolts were
used in warfare until the 1600s. A wad of
hemp or flax was soaked in a flammable
substance, fixed beneath the
arrowhead, and then
lit just before the
arrow was shot.

Stirrup (foot strap)

Backsight

Sighting bead

**BACKSIGHT**
Backsights, situated in the middle
of bullet and stone crossbows, had a
number of apertures (openings) for
sighting to different distances. The
backsight in this weapon is lying
flat and would have been pulled
upright for firing.

Double bowstring
with leather
pouch

**SIGHTING BEAD**
A movable sighting bead
hung between the
foresight pillars of
bullet-firing crossbows.

Nock

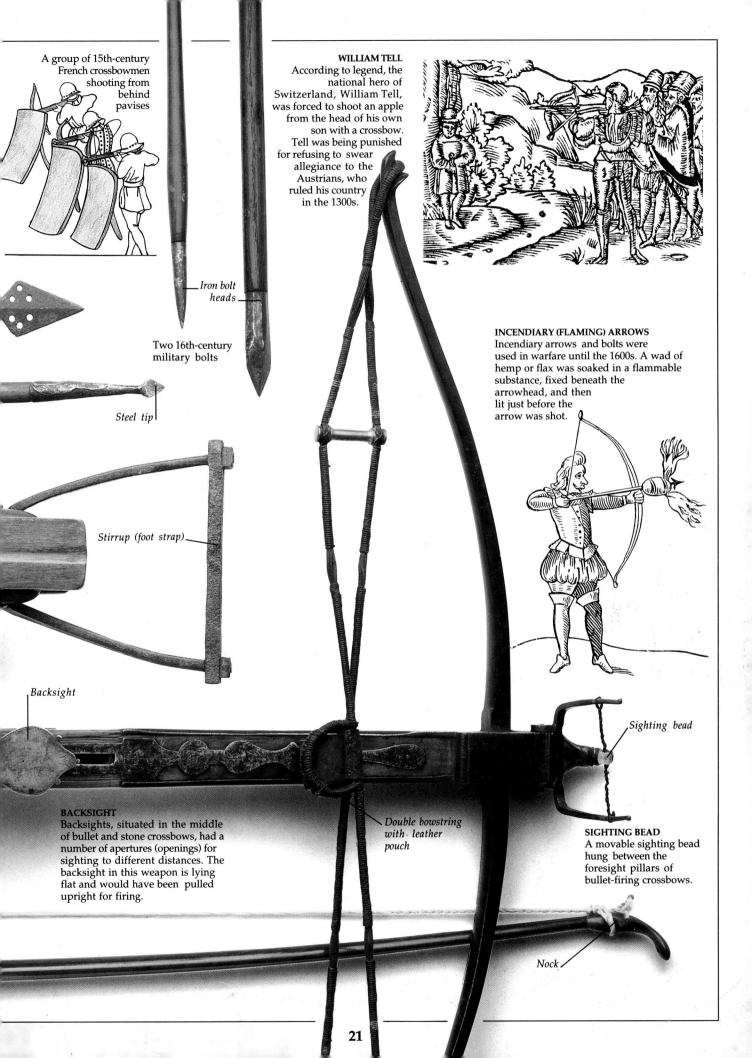

# Axes, daggers and knives

AXES, DAGGERS, AND KNIVES have been used as weapons since prehistoric times (pp. 6-7). At first, axe heads were made of stone or bronze, but by the Middle Ages, they were usually made of steel or iron, and often had additional spikes or projections to make them even more formidable. Although daggers and knives seem similar to one another, a dagger, with its two sharp edges running into a point, is essentially a stabbing weapon, while a knife with its single-edged blade is usually used for cutting. By looking at a selection of axes, daggers, and knives from all over the world it is possible to see how different countries produce blades and shafts to suit their own special requirements and cultures.

19th-century American infantryman carrying a bowie knife

**RING KNIFE**
Worn as a ring around the user's forefinger, this curved knife can be found amoung the Bantu-speaking peoples of the Lake Turkana region in Tanzania, East Africa.

Ring placed around forefinger

Iron blade

**THROWING KNIFE**
This African throwing knife (pp. 8-9) comes from Zaire, West Africa. When thrown, the knife turns around its center of gravity so that it will inflict a wound on an opponent whatever its point of impact.

Wooden hilt bound in leather and copper

**STABBING AXE** *below*
An unusual-looking axe made by the Matabele people of Zimbabwe, southern Africa. As the top of the haft is angled in line with the pointed end of the blade, the axe can be used for both stabbing and chopping.

Worn in palm of hand

**STABBING KNIFE** *left*
An unusual type of knife, worn in the palm of the hand and then thrust forward by the user. It was made in West Africa by northern Nigerian tribespeople.

**AZTEC DAGGER**
The Aztecs, Middle American Indians who once dominated Mexico, made this flint dagger with a mosaic handle.

**NAGA WAR AXE** *above*
The *dao* is an impressive-looking all-purpose weapon used by the former headhunting peoples from the Naga Hills of Assam, India, in their intertribal warfare.

Long bamboo haft partly bound with rings of plaited cane

**FOLDING KNIFE** *above*
In this late 19th-century Spanish knife the blade folds back to sit partly within the hilt. The blade was locked into place by a steel spring in the hilt.

Hilt made of horn with brass ferrule

**EXECUTIONER'S AXE**
The large, heavy, two-handed axes used for beheadings were made only in central and northern Europe.

Plume of dyed animal hair

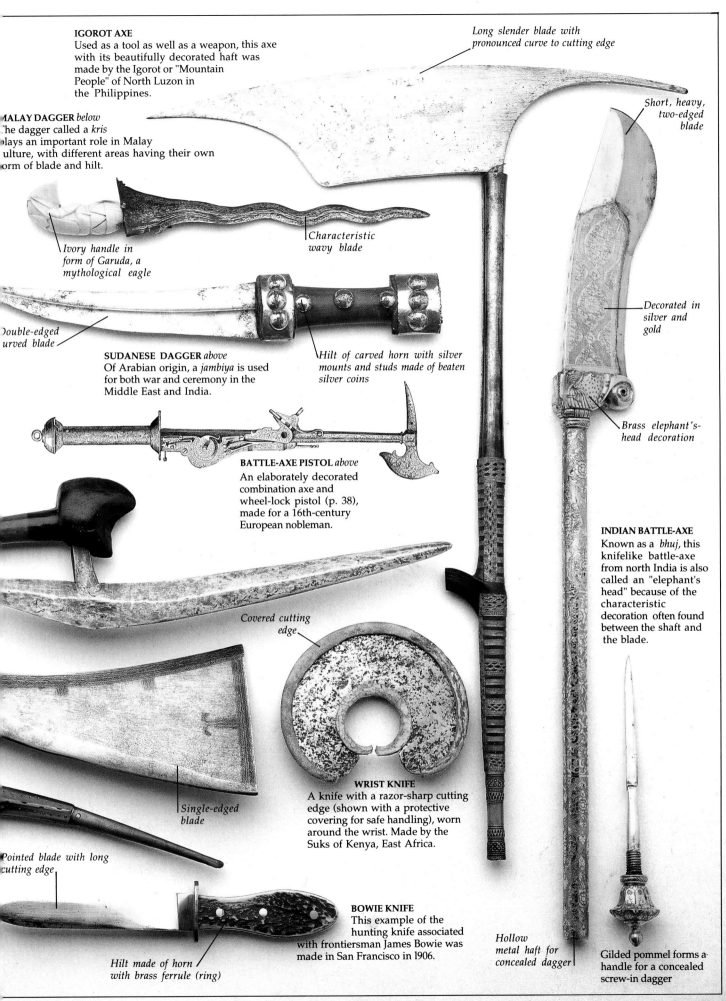

**IGOROT AXE**
Used as a tool as well as a weapon, this axe with its beautifully decorated haft was made by the Igorot or "Mountain People" of North Luzon in the Philippines.

*Long slender blade with pronounced curve to cutting edge*

*Short, heavy, two-edged blade*

**MALAY DAGGER** *below*
The dagger called a *kris* plays an important role in Malay culture, with different areas having their own form of blade and hilt.

*Ivory handle in form of Garuda, a mythological eagle*

*Characteristic wavy blade*

*Decorated in silver and gold*

*Double-edged curved blade*

*Hilt of carved horn with silver mounts and studs made of beaten silver coins*

**SUDANESE DAGGER** *above*
Of Arabian origin, a *jambiya* is used for both war and ceremony in the Middle East and India.

*Brass elephant's-head decoration*

**BATTLE-AXE PISTOL** *above*
An elaborately decorated combination axe and wheel-lock pistol (p. 38), made for a 16th-century European nobleman.

**INDIAN BATTLE-AXE**
Known as a *bhuj*, this knifelike battle-axe from north India is also called an "elephant's head" because of the characteristic decoration often found between the shaft and the blade.

*Covered cutting edge*

*Single-edged blade*

**WRIST KNIFE**
A knife with a razor-sharp cutting edge (shown with a protective covering for safe handling), worn around the wrist. Made by the Suks of Kenya, East Africa.

*Pointed blade with long cutting edge*

**BOWIE KNIFE**
This example of the hunting knife associated with frontiersman James Bowie was made in San Francisco in 1906.

*Hilt made of horn with brass ferrule (ring)*

*Hollow metal haft for concealed dagger*

*Gilded pommel forms a handle for a concealed screw-in dagger*

# Plate and mail armor

CHAIN MAIL - ARMOR made from linked iron or steel rings - was the main type of armor worn from the Celtic period in the 6th century B.C. (pp. 10-11) until the 13th century. By then knights found mail armor not only uncomfortable to wear but also inadequate protection against weapons such as war hammers and two-handed swords. At first plate armor, which was gradually introduced in the 13th century, was simply added to mail armor. But from the 1400s until the coming of firearms in the 1600s, knights went to war entirely encased in suits of plate armor.

**EARLY LEG DEFENSE**
An Italian relief, c.1289, showing medieval leather leg protection.

An armored knight in an attitude of devotion, c. 1290

**MAIL SHIRT**
This Oriental mail shirt is made of solid rings - made without any join. European mail was usually riveted - each ring end flattened and linked by a rivet.

**WAR HAMMER, c. 1580** *right*
This armor-piercing French war hammer originally had a longer shaft for use by knights fighting on foot.

**MEDIEVAL KNIGHT IN MAIL ARMOR**
A window in the Palace of Westminster, London.

**A JOUST IN FRANCE, c. 1446**
Until the 16th century, knights wore ordinary battle armor for jousting at tournaments (pp. 30-31).

*Long sharp point at back of weapon balanced by blunt claws in front*

**BREASTPLATE, c. 1570**
Made by a well-known Italian armorer, this light, strong, one-piece breastplate is a technically perfect piece of plate armor. Its style imitates the shape of a 16th-century doublet (close-fitting jacket).

*Roped turns for deflecting edged weapons*

*Straps for attaching to a backplate*

*Decorated with engraved and gilded heavenly figures*

**GERMAN KNIGHT**
A colored engraving of a fully-armed knight, drawn in about 1500. He is dressed in Maximilian armor, which was both heavier and rounder than earlier styles of plate armor.

*Lance rest for tilting (pp. 30-31)*

*Straps for attaching metal-plate skirts to longer plates called tassets (p. 26)*

*Back plate of jointed steel plates, the last of which is shaped to the knuckles*

*One plate, the cuff, covers the wrist*

**GAUNTLET, c. 1580** *left*
Made in north Germany, this gauntlet - the piece of armor that protected the hand and wrist - shows the detail and skill with which high-quality plate armor was made.

**SABATON, c. 1550** *below*
As with the gauntlet (above), the part of the armor that protected the foot had to allow for maximum movement, so it had well-made articulated (jointed) plates along the length of the foot.

**AN ARMORER'S WORKSHOP IN INNSBRUCK, AUSTRIA, c. 1517**
An especially strong and heavy type of armor, made in Germany and Austria during the 16th century, was called Maximilian armor after the Hapsburg emperor Maximilian I. In this engraving Maximilan is visiting his chief armorer.

*Exaggerated long-pointed toe cap, articulated where foot bends*

# A suit of armor

BY THE MIDDLE OF THE 15TH century a fully armed knight was virtually encased in plate armor. However, due to the skill of the late medieval armorer, he was not as restricted as he might appear; the armor joints were designed to permit a large amount of movement. The suit of armor on these pages, belonging to an early 16th-century knight, was made in an Italian workshop - the northern Italians and the southern Germans were the most celebrated armorers in Europe.

*Large visor, with eye slits and vents for breathing, was designed to slide up onto the wearer's brow*

*Visor hinge and pivot*

*Leather strap and buckle for connecting breastplate to backplate*

*Vents for breathing*

**NECK DEFENSE**
From the 13th century all types of armor had gorgets (collar plates).

**PROTECTING THE HEAD** *right*
The knight's head was protected by a helmet. This particular type, a close helmet (p. 28), fits to the shape of the face and has connecting neck-guard plates (known as gorget plates).

*Neck edge and armpit has turns for deflecting edged weapons*

*Gorget plates to overlap with gorget*

*Strap for buckling skirt to tassets*

*Tassets made of jointed steel plates permitting freedom of movement at the waist*

**ST. GEORGE KILLING THE DRAGON** *left*
It is best not to study paintings too closely when looking for accurate depictions of medieval armor as the artist often romanticized even contemporary armor.

**BREASTPLATE SECTION OF CUIRASS**
The cuirass, the armor that covered the torso, was made of a breastplate and a backplate connected to each other by straps. Extending from this breastplate are skirts and tassets - armor to protect the abdomen and upper thighs.

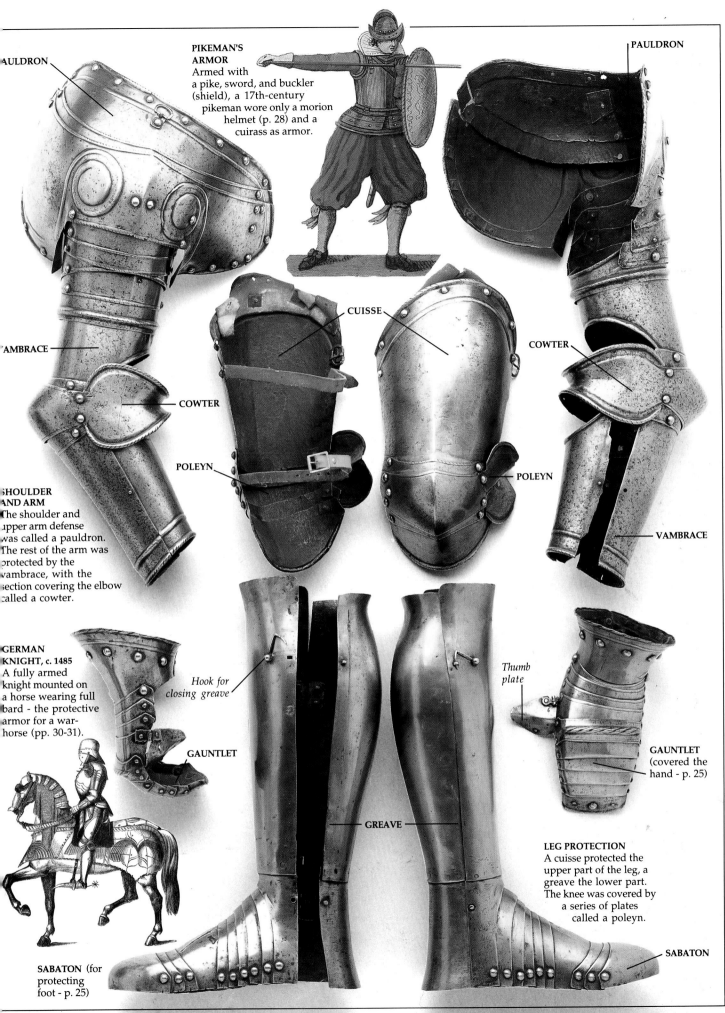

**AULDRON**

**PIKEMAN'S ARMOR**
Armed with a pike, sword, and buckler (shield), a 17th-century pikeman wore only a morion helmet (p. 28) and a cuirass as armor.

**PAULDRON**

**VAMBRACE**

**CUISSE**

**COWTER**

**COWTER**

**POLEYN**

**POLEYN**

**VAMBRACE**

**SHOULDER AND ARM**
The shoulder and upper arm defense was called a pauldron. The rest of the arm was protected by the vambrace, with the section covering the elbow called a cowter.

**GERMAN KNIGHT, c. 1485**
A fully armed knight mounted on a horse wearing full bard - the protective armor for a war-horse (pp. 30-31).

*Hook for closing greave*

**GAUNTLET**

*Thumb plate*

**GAUNTLET**
(covered the hand - p. 25)

**GREAVE**

**LEG PROTECTION**
A cuisse protected the upper part of the leg, a greave the lower part. The knee was covered by a series of plates called a poleyn.

**SABATON** (for protecting foot - p. 25)

**SABATON**

27

# Helmets

**W**ARRIORS HAVE WORN protective helmets since the Bronze Age (pp. 10-11). But in the Middle Ages, helmets became considerably larger so as to give greater protection to the face and neck. The heaviest and largest was the *heaume* or helm, an enormous helmet which a knight carried on his saddle when not fighting. In the late Middle Ages, helmets called bascinets were fastened to the rest of the body armor by screws and chains, and knights also wore helmets with pivotable sections, such as the close helmet. A later development was the smaller, lighter helmet (the morion and the pot helmets). After the 1600s steel helmets were mostly replaced by military headgear made of leather, brass, felt, or fur.

13th-century helm with two eye slits and breathing holes

**FLAT-TOPPED HELM**
A 19th-century reproduction of a German *heaume* or helm, the type of helmet worn by the Crusaders and other European knights from the early 1200s. Its reinforcing strips are cross shaped.

**ARCHER, c. 1290** *right*
A mounted archer wearing a conical helm.

*Skull*

*Comb*

*Lifting peg*

*Visor with eye slits and breathing vents*

*High comb*

*Plume holder*

*Gorget (neck plate)*

*Down-turned brim curving up to sharply pointed peak*

*Originally had leather chin strap tied under chin with lace*

**CLOSE HELMET, c. 1520-30**
The most characteristic helmet of the 16th century was the close helmet (above and left), which unlike earlier helmets was shaped to the chin and had an attached gorget (p. 26).

**COMB-MORION, c. 1580**
A comb-morion was worn by infantry (as left), especially archers and musketeers, who found an open style of helmet more convenient when taking aim.

**PIKEMAN"S HELMET** *below*
17th-century pikemen's helmets had flat brims and laminated cheekguards.

**Three pieces of steel welded together**

**Eye slit**

**Breathing holes**

**Stud for attaching visor**

### CONICAL HELM, c. 1370
After the 1350s the helm was mainly used for tilting (pp. 30-31). This (19th-century reproduction) helm would probably have been worn on top of a bascinet (right), placing an enormous weight on the knight's shoulders.

*Guard-chain or safety chain - when helm not worn, it was often carried by chain*

14th-century knights wearing bascinets and a common soldier wearing a helmet called a kettle-hat (above)

### BASCINET, c. 1370
Between 1350 and 1450 the most popular type of helmet was the bascinet. Visors - hinged plates for protecting the face - were introduced about 1300. This German bascinet would originally have had a type of visor known as a *klappvisier*, which was hinged to a curved, vertical bar attached by two studs to the brow of the bascinet.

*Laminated neck guard riveted to helmet's skull and partially shaped to neck*

*Originally covered in cloth, probably velvet*

**Sliding nasal bar**

17th-century musketeer wearing ordinary civilian hat

### ON HAT, c. 1640-50
n unusual helmet is this high- owned iron hat with a sliding sal bar, occasionally worn by rsemen during the English vil War (1642-48). Originally vered in material and with a plume, looked like a civilian hat of the time.

*Face guard formed of three vertical bars*

*Cheek- pieces*

### "LOBSTER-TAILED" POT, c. 1630-50
A type of helmet worn in the mid-17th century originated in Germany, where it was called a *zischagge*. The English variation, worn by cavalry during the Civil War of 1642-48 (right), was known as the English pot or "lobster- tailed pot." It had a face guard, neck guard and hinged cheek- pieces (left and above).

# Tilting armor

THE EARLIEST TOURNAMENTS - mock battles between mounted knights - probably began in the 1100s as a form of rehearsal for war. But by the 1400s tournaments had evolved into important and colorful social events at which knights displayed their fighting skills and courage before their monarch and their peers. The mock battles became known as jousts, and each joust started with two mounted knights charging each other with lances across a barrier known as a tilt. As tilting required additional protection for the left or target side of the body, special tilting armor was made for knights taking part in tournaments.

A French knight
tilting with a lance

**COATS OF ARMS**
Tournament contestants were identified by the personal insignia displayed on their shields and tunics. Originally shown on the surcoats worn over chain mail, the insignia became known as coats of arms.

**TILTING HELMET, c. 1630** *left*
By the 17th century, tournaments had become chiefly displays of horsemanship. Tilting armor became more showy, as can be seen by this bronze tilting helmet with its grotesque human face mask.

**A JOUSTING CONTEST** *above*
By the 16th century, tournaments were accompanied by much formal pageantry. The field, or lists, was enclosed by barriers and overlooked by pavilions where royalty and other notables could watch. This depiction of a tournament shows King Henry VIII tilting with one of his knights, watched by his queen.

**TILTING SPUR** *below*
Horsemen wear spurs on their heels to urge their horses into action. By the 1500s tilting spurs often had rowels with especially strong and sharp spikes to prod their horses into a charge.

*Rowel*

**HORSE ARMOR** *below*
The complete set of armor that protected a war-horse in battle was called the bard. In a tournament the horse usually wore only the section of the bard known as the chanfron, a series of metal plates that protected its forehead and face. At the center of the chanfron there was nearly always a shield with a spike projecting from the middle of it.

**DON QUIXOTE TILTING AT WINDMILLS**
In the novel *Don Quixote* (written by the Spanish author Cervantes in 1605-14), an old knight's belief in the chivalric romances he has read leads him into a series of unusual adventures. During his travels Don Quixote tilts at windmills, imagining them to be giants.

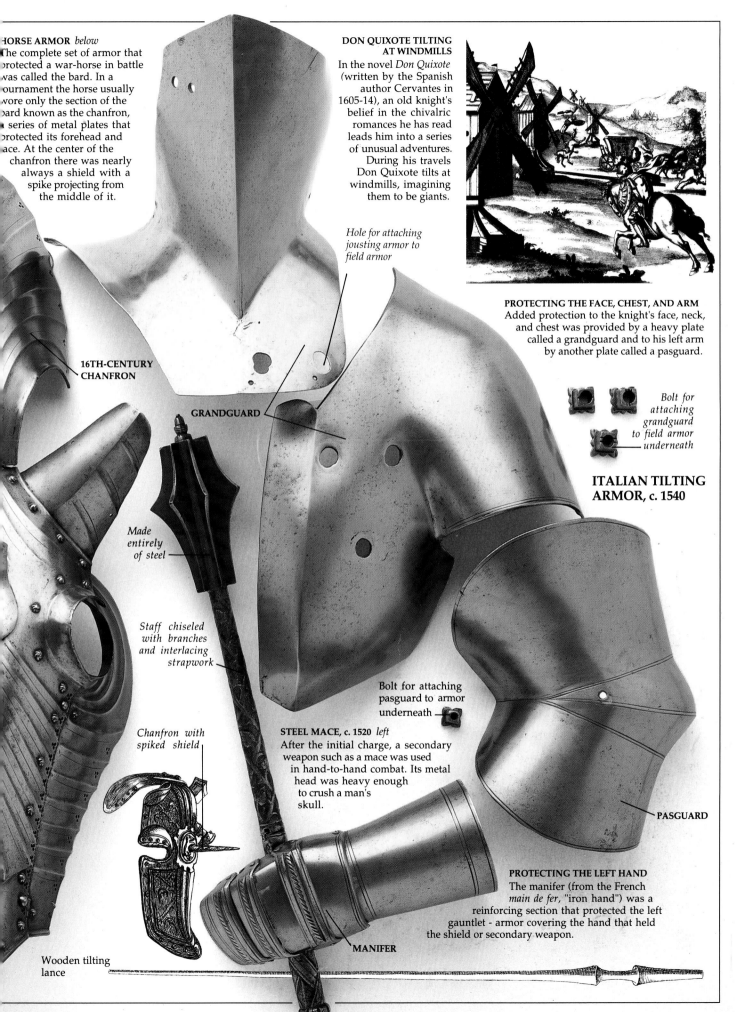

**PROTECTING THE FACE, CHEST, AND ARM**
Added protection to the knight's face, neck, and chest was provided by a heavy plate called a grandguard and to his left arm by another plate called a pasguard.

*Hole for attaching jousting armor to field armor*

**16TH-CENTURY CHANFRON**

**GRANDGUARD**

*Bolt for attaching grandguard to field armor underneath*

**ITALIAN TILTING ARMOR, c. 1540**

*Made entirely of steel*

*Staff chiseled with branches and interlacing strapwork*

*Chanfron with spiked shield*

Bolt for attaching pasguard to armor underneath

**STEEL MACE, c. 1520** *left*
After the initial charge, a secondary weapon such as a mace was used in hand-to-hand combat. Its metal head was heavy enough to crush a man's skull.

**PASGUARD**

**PROTECTING THE LEFT HAND**
The manifer (from the French *main de fer*, "iron hand") was a reinforcing section that protected the left gauntlet - armor covering the hand that held the shield or secondary weapon.

**MANIFER**

Wooden tilting lance

# An Indian warrior

F OR MANY CENTURIES the Persians were the supreme craftsmen of Asia, and Oriental arms and armor were dominated by Persian styles and workmanship. We know, for example, from early Indian art that, except for a type of shield, the Indian people did not develop their own armor until the 16th century when the Mogul invaders introduced Persian-style body armor and weapons. Although some Indian weapons such as the matchlock musket were derived from European firearms, the arms and armor of the north Indian warrior shown on these pages were remarkably similar to that of a Persian or Turkish warrior.

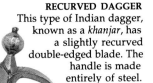

A 19th-century engraving of a scimitar

*Carved ivory grip*

*Short straight quillons (extended cross guards)*

*Colored enamel decoration*

*Double-edged, watered-steel blade*

**MOGUL BATTLE SCENE** *below*
The Moguls were Muslim warriors who founded a great empire in India, which lasted from the 16th to the 19th century. In this 17th-century Mogul miniature, the warriors are wearing characteristic north Indian armor and weapons.

*Watered-steel blade*

*Sling hoops in decorated enamel*

*Velvet lining*

**LIGHTWEIGHT SABER** *right*
The *shamshir*, a light saber, is a classic Indian sword. Originating in Persia, the weapon spread to India, and eventually to Europe, where it became known as the scimitar.

**FIGHTING AXE**
A popular weapon among Indian warriors was the *tabar*, an all-steel axe (pp. 34-35). This particular type of *tabar* has a sharp pick opposite a crescent-shaped blade.

## CIRCULAR STEEL SHIELD *below*

By the 18th century, Indian and Persian soldiers were using a round shield (*dhal* or *spar*) made of steel or hide (pp. 34-35). Four bosses (studs) covered the attachment of the handles for carrying the shield on the left arm.

*Made of watered-steel with chiseled and gilded decoration, north Indian, c. 19th century*

## INDIAN WARRIORS

Photograph, taken in 1857, of Rajput warriors. They are armed with a *dhal*, *tulwar*, and *bandukh toradar* (matchlock musket).

*Spike socket (spike missing)*

## NORTH INDIAN HELMET

Known as a *top*, an Indian helmet had mail curtains called aventails descending to the shoulders. The helmet was secured under the chin with a braid tie.

*Socket for feather or tinsel plume (plume missing)*

*Sliding nasal bar for protecting nose*

*Aventail to protect the neck, shoulders, and part of the face*

*Mail shoulder straps with metal clasps*

## ARM GUARD *below*

The tubular vambrace or *dastana* was fastened to the arm with straps. The chain-mail extension is to protect the hand.

## RECTANGULAR BREASTPLATE *right*

The Indian cuirass, known as a *char aina* (Persian for "four mirrors"), consisted of a light breastplate, a backplate, and two side plates, all of which were shaped to fit on top of the warrior's mail shirt.

*Wooden shamshir scabbard bound in tooled leather*

*Decorated in gold and silver false damascene*

*Lined gold damascened trellis pattern*

# Indian weapons

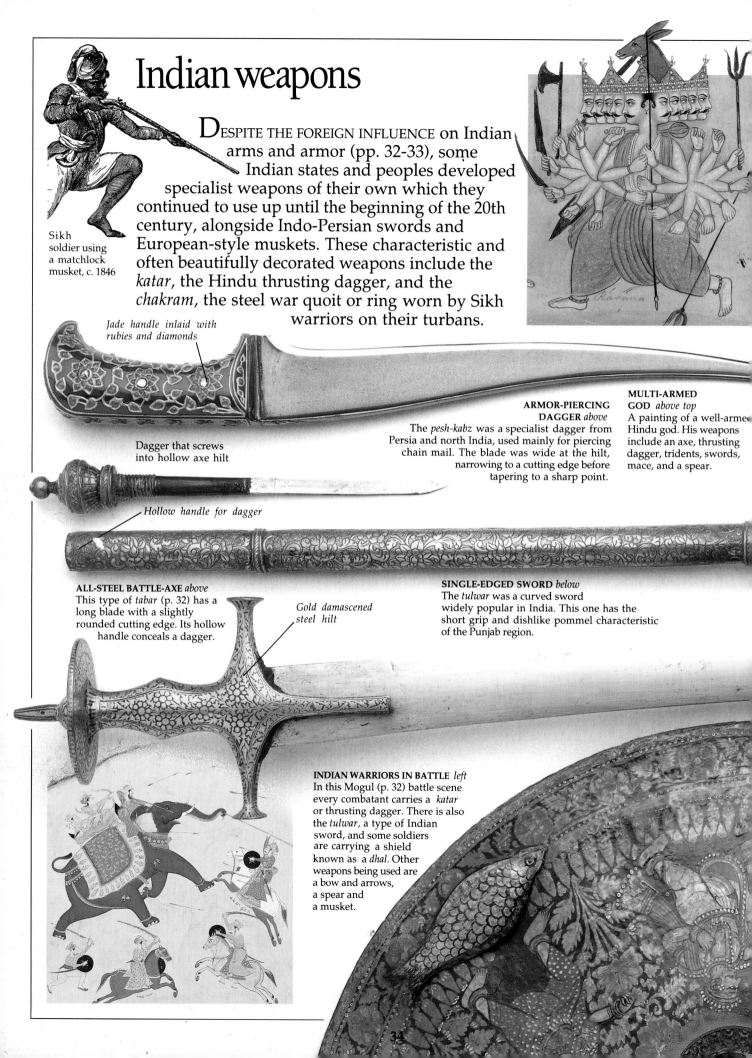

DESPITE THE FOREIGN INFLUENCE on Indian arms and armor (pp. 32-33), some Indian states and peoples developed specialist weapons of their own which they continued to use up until the beginning of the 20th century, alongside Indo-Persian swords and European-style muskets. These characteristic and often beautifully decorated weapons include the *katar*, the Hindu thrusting dagger, and the *chakram*, the steel war quoit or ring worn by Sikh warriors on their turbans.

Sikh soldier using a matchlock musket, c. 1846

Jade handle inlaid with rubies and diamonds

Dagger that screws into hollow axe hilt

Hollow handle for dagger

**ARMOR-PIERCING DAGGER** *above*
The *pesh-kabz* was a specialist dagger from Persia and north India, used mainly for piercing chain mail. The blade was wide at the hilt, narrowing to a cutting edge before tapering to a sharp point.

**MULTI-ARMED GOD** *above top*
A painting of a well-armed Hindu god. His weapons include an axe, thrusting dagger, tridents, swords, mace, and a spear.

**ALL-STEEL BATTLE-AXE** *above*
This type of *tabar* (p. 32) has a long blade with a slightly rounded cutting edge. Its hollow handle conceals a dagger.

Gold damascened steel hilt

**SINGLE-EDGED SWORD** *below*
The *tulwar* was a curved sword widely popular in India. This one has the short grip and dishlike pommel characteristic of the Punjab region.

**INDIAN WARRIORS IN BATTLE** *left*
In this Mogul (p. 32) battle scene every combatant carries a *katar* or thrusting dagger. There is also the *tulwar*, a type of Indian sword, and some soldiers are carrying a shield known as a *dhal*. Other weapons being used are a bow and arrows, a spear and a musket.

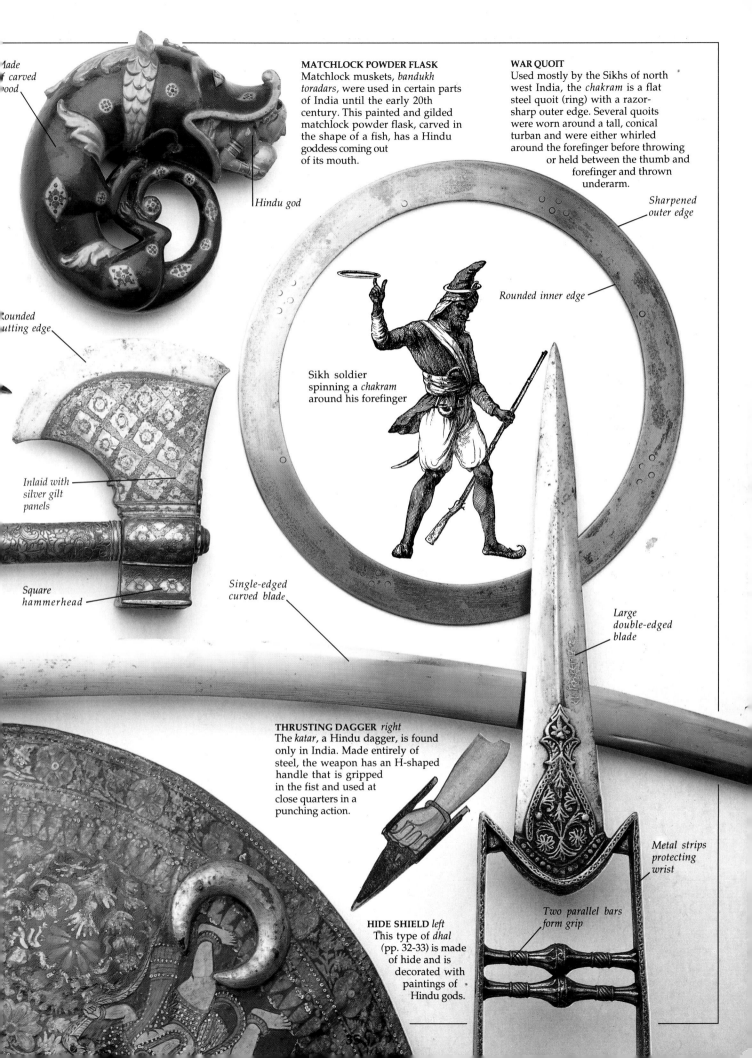

*Made of carved wood*

**MATCHLOCK POWDER FLASK**
Matchlock muskets, *bandukh toradars*, were used in certain parts of India until the early 20th century. This painted and gilded matchlock powder flask, carved in the shape of a fish, has a Hindu goddess coming out of its mouth.

*Hindu god*

**WAR QUOIT**
Used mostly by the Sikhs of north west India, the *chakram* is a flat steel quoit (ring) with a razor-sharp outer edge. Several quoits were worn around a tall, conical turban and were either whirled around the forefinger before throwing or held between the thumb and forefinger and thrown underarm.

*Sharpened outer edge*

*Rounded inner edge*

*Rounded cutting edge*

*Inlaid with silver gilt panels*

*Square hammerhead*

*Single-edged curved blade*

Sikh soldier spinning a *chakram* around his forefinger

*Large double-edged blade*

**THRUSTING DAGGER** *right*
The *katar*, a Hindu dagger, is found only in India. Made entirely of steel, the weapon has an H-shaped handle that is gripped in the fist and used at close quarters in a punching action.

*Metal strips protecting wrist*

*Two parallel bars form grip*

**HIDE SHIELD** *left*
This type of *dhal* (pp. 32-33) is made of hide and is decorated with paintings of Hindu gods.

# A Japanese samurai

A *tsuba* (or sword guard)

J APANESE WEAPONS and armor are unique. Developed over many centuries, the armor is far more decorative than its European or Middle Eastern counterparts, especially the highly ornamented type worn by the warriors known as samurai (Japanese for "soldier"), whose code of honor dominated Japanese military life from the 12th century until 1868, when the samurai class was abolished. Japanese arms are equally well constructed, especially the swords, without doubt the finest ever made.

A *wakizashi* scabbard (a *saya*) made of lacquered wood (below)

Wooden sheath for spear head

Blade made by covering a soft iron core with layers of steel

Kabuto *helmet with horn-shaped crest*

Metal collar to protect point of junction in a decorative manner

Large crayfish design in black lacquer

Ornamentation with mosaic design made of mother-of-pearl

Silken cord for securing sword to girdle

Flecked lacquer sheath

Lacquered hilt

*Known as tsuba, Japanese sword guards are collectors' items (above left)*

Hilt made of wood covered with fish skin and bound with flat braid

**FOOT SOLDIER** *above*
This 19th-century foot soldier is wearing a light cuirass (p. 26) or *haramaki*. Designed mainly for foot soldiers, the *haramaki* covered the soldier's chest and sides with additional skirts (*kasazuri*) protecting his lower torso.

**DAGGER** *above*
An example of the typical Japanese dagger (the *tanto*) with its single-edged blade.

**SPEAR** *left*
Short-bladed spears (*yari*) were carried by horsemen. Foot soldiers carried longer-bladed *yari* (see right).

**SHORT SWORD** *left*
A samurai carried both a short and a long sword. This 17th-century sword is a *wakizashi*, a short sword used not only as an additional fighting sword, but also for seppuku, the ritual suicide.

**SCABBARD FITTINGS**
A small knife known as the *kozuka* (left) and a skewer, the *kogai* (far left), were carried on either side of *tanto* scabbards.

*Hand guard or half-gauntlet, known as the tetsu-gai, with leather lining and loops for fingers*

**SAMURAI COMBAT** *left*
This early 19th-century print shows a sword fight between two samurai fighting with *katana*, long fighting swords. Their secondary swords, *wakizashi*, are tucked through the girdles around their waists.

*Opening (the tehen) for warrior's pigtail to pass through*

*Helmet bowl (hachi) made of riveted plates*

*Wings or protective flaps known as the fukigayeshi*

*Decorated with brass and lacquer*

*The maidate - the socket for the helmet crest*

*Cord for attaching mask to helmet*

*Hempen mustache*

*Gorget (nowdawa) fastened at the back of the neck by cords*

*Laminated neck guard (shikoro)*

**WAR MASK** *above*
Warriors wore different types of war masks or *menpo*, such as this half-mask with a nose-piece called a *mempo*. Masks not only secured the helmet firmly to the head but also gave the wearer a more frightening appearance.

*Made of silk overlaid with chain mail connecting metal plates*

Japanese general wearing a *kabuto* helmet with a helmet crest or *kasajirushi*

**SAMURAI HELMET**
Known generally as *kabuto*, Japanese helmets developed from prehistoric times until the 19th century, with each period having its own distinct features and design. The *kabuto* was secured to the head with cords attached to the brim.

**ARMORED SLEEVE** *below*
A type of vambrace (p. 27), the armored sleeve (*kote*) protected the arm from spears and swords. Made of close-fitting material, it was laced over the arm and tied around the chest.

# Early firearms

ALTHOUGH GUNPOWDER was used by soldiers in Europe in the 14th century, it was not until the 16th century that small arms began to fulfill their potential. Wooden stocks now helped the firer to aim, absorb the recoil, and hold the hot barrel; an ignition mechanism or lock let him fire at just the right moment. The simple matchlock plunged a smoldering slow-match into the priming pan at the touch of a trigger. A later form of ignition, the wheel-lock, went one stage further, by generating sparks at the moment of firing. As it was too expensive to replace the matchlock entirely for the common soldier, both these systems were used until they were replaced by the more efficient flintlock (pp. 40-41).

**LIGHT CAVALRYMAN**
Wheel-lock pistols were the first small arms carried by cavalrymen.

*Cock or "dog" holding iron pyrites*

*Iron butt cap*

*Stock inlaid with brass and mother-of-pearl*

*Wheel*

*Stock shaped to fit wheel*

*"March, and with your Musket carry your rest"*

*"Poise your Musket"*

*"Shorten your scouring stick"*

*"Try your Match"*

*"Give Fire"*

**LOADING SEQUENCE**
Early muzzleloaders may appear simple, but they had to be loaded in strict sequence to prevent misfiring or personal injury. On the left are a few of the loading and firing actions taught to soldiers using these early firearms.

## The matchlock

This matchlock is a typical infantry musket of the early 17th century. The pan cover was opened just before taking aim. On pulling the trigger, the lock thrust the tip of the match into the pan to ignite the priming, and a flash went through a small touchhole in the barrel wall to set off the main charge.

**OBSCURING THE TARGET**
One drawback of the original black gunpowder was the dense white smoke it produced, which often obscured the target and made aiming difficult.

*Priming pan and cover*

*Rope slow-match*

*Wooden stock*

*Trigger guard*

*Trigger*

**GERMAN MATCHLOCK MUSKET, c. early 17th century**

# The wheel-lock

This lock produced sparks by holding a bunch of iron pyrites against the notched edge of a spinning wheel, which extended into the bottom of the priming pan. Just below the pan was a square spindle on which a key was fitted. As the key was turned a short chain attached to the mainspring caused it to wind up. After the "dog" or cock was lowered into the pan, the wheel was released. It spun against the pyrites and showered sparks into the pan, setting off the priming and main charge.

**RANGE OF FIRE**
The advantage of firearms was that they could hit an enemy before he could use a bladed weapon, such as a lance.

Wooden ramrod

*Most early small arms were muzzleloaders - loaded from the front or muzzle end*

## WHEEL-LOCK PISTOL, north European, c. 17th century

**MUSKET RESTS**
Heavy matchlock muskets were fired from forked rests.

**MUSKETEER**
Engraving of a musketeer with a smoldering match for his musket and a horn powder flask.

*Engraving of David and Goliath*

*Made of flattened cow horn*

Pure lead pistol balls

**POWDER FLASK**
For safety's sake, powder flasks had to be made of non-iron materials such as cow horn. This powder flask, dating from 1608, would have been worn by a musketeer in the fashion shown in the engraving on the left.

*Spout doubles as measure*

**BREASTPLATE** *right*
Armor had to be thickened to resist small-arms fire, and so less of it could be worn. This older, thinner breastplate has been pierced by a musket ball fired at the wearer during the English Civil War of 1642-48.

*Black gunpowder*

# Flintlock firearms

**M**ORE RELIABLE THAN THE MATCHLOCK and cheaper than the wheel-lock (pp. 38-39), flintlock ignition was used on most European and American firearms from the late 17th century until the 1830s. Probably invented in France by Martin Le Bourgeoys in the 1620s, the flintlock mechanism could be set in two positions - one for firing and one for safety. With its basic design improved by only a few details, the flintlock ignition not only dominated the battlefields of all the major wars of that period but was an important civilian weapon as well, used for dueling (pp. 46-47), self-defense (pp. 48-49), and game shooting. Many of these weapons showed the highest standards of craftsmanship.

*The pirate Long John Silver in Robert Louis Stevenson's Treasure Island*

**SPORTSMAN SHOOTING GAME**
As the hunter fires his flintlock "fowling piece", the flash from the pan can be clearly seen.

## Loading and firing a flintlock (also pp. 46-47)

1 Set lock to "half-cock" safety position.
2 Pour correct amount of powder from powder flask (p. 39) or cartridge down barrel.
3 Ram ball, wrapped in its patch (p. 46) or cartridge down barrel with ramrod.
4 Pour small amount of powder from powder flask into priming pan.
5 Close pan cover.
6 Set lock to "full-cock" position and fire.

*Musket ball*

**MUSKET CARTRIDGE POUCH**
Each paper cartridge contains powder and ball for one shot.

*Lock*  *Pan cover*

*D·EGG*

*Priming pan*

*Brown walnut stock*

*Brass butt cap*

*Socket*

**FLINTLOCK MUSKET**
This late 18th-century India Pattern musket comes from the family of longarms sometimes known as Brown Bess muskets. These muskets were so strong, simple to use, and relatively reliable, they remained the main British infantry weapon from the 1720s to the 1840s.

**SOCKET BAYONET**
This bayonet was designed to accompany Brown Bess muskets. Most European and North American armies used triangular-bladed bayonets with a socket to fit over the muzzle.

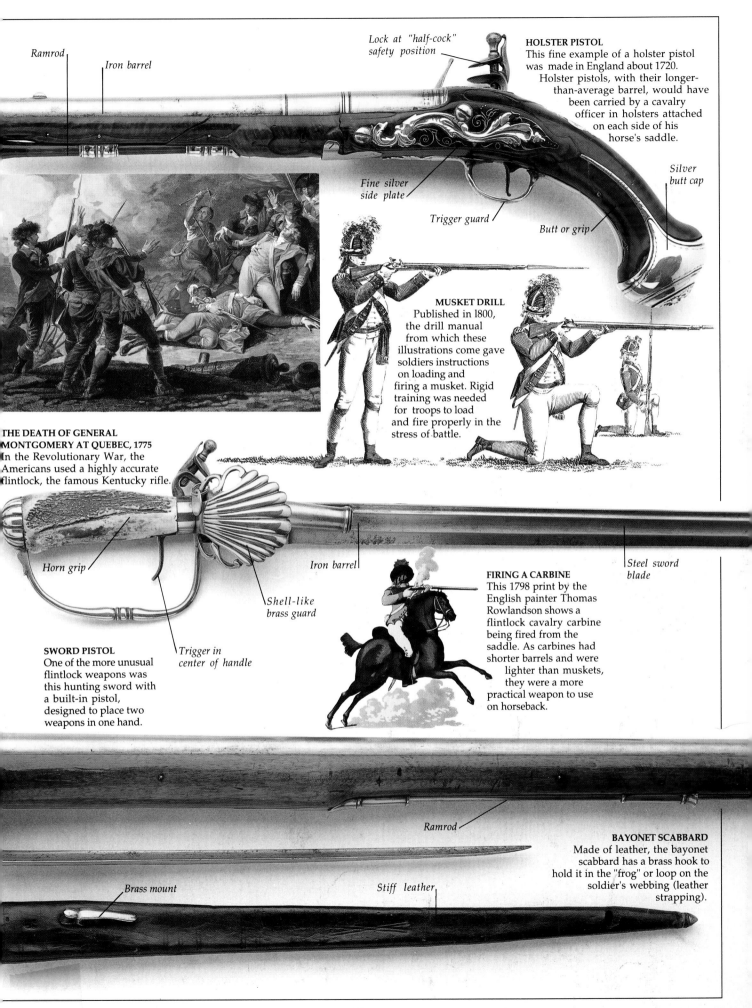

_Ramrod_

_Iron barrel_

_Lock at "half-cock" safety position_

**HOLSTER PISTOL**
This fine example of a holster pistol was made in England about 1720. Holster pistols, with their longer-than-average barrel, would have been carried by a cavalry officer in holsters attached on each side of his horse's saddle.

_Fine silver side plate_

_Trigger guard_

_Silver butt cap_

_Butt or grip_

**MUSKET DRILL**
Published in 1800, the drill manual from which these illustrations come gave soldiers instructions on loading and firing a musket. Rigid training was needed for troops to load and fire properly in the stress of battle.

**THE DEATH OF GENERAL MONTGOMERY AT QUEBEC, 1775**
In the Revolutionary War, the Americans used a highly accurate flintlock, the famous Kentucky rifle.

_Horn grip_

_Shell-like brass guard_

_Iron barrel_

_Steel sword blade_

**FIRING A CARBINE**
This 1798 print by the English painter Thomas Rowlandson shows a flintlock cavalry carbine being fired from the saddle. As carbines had shorter barrels and were lighter than muskets, they were a more practical weapon to use on horseback.

**SWORD PISTOL**
One of the more unusual flintlock weapons was this hunting sword with a built-in pistol, designed to place two weapons in one hand.

_Trigger in center of handle_

_Ramrod_

**BAYONET SCABBARD**
Made of leather, the bayonet scabbard has a brass hook to hold it in the "frog" or loop on the soldier's webbing (leather strapping).

_Brass mount_

_Stiff leather_

# Dueling swords

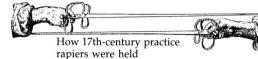

*How 17th-century practice rapiers were held*

Aを LTHOUGH THEY WERE FRIGHTENING WEAPONS, the swords taken into battle by medieval knights and foot soldiers were relatively simple (pp. 16-17). However, during the 16th century sword designs changed, and some blades became narrower, longer, and more pointed. These swords, known as rapiers, were designed for well-off gentlemen and aristocrats, not only to defend themselves against casual attacks but also to take part in formal prearranged sword fights known as duels. The art of fighting with a rapier became known as fencing, and as fencing techniques became more sophisticated, sword guards became more complex with the need to protect a civilian's unarmored hand. The greatest swordsmiths of this period came from Toledo in Spain, Milan in Italy, and Solingen in Germany, and many of the weapons they produced are artistically superb examples of the craft of sword making. By the 1650s, rapiers were being replaced as dress swords and dueling swords by a lighter, shorter type of sword with a simpler guard known as a smallsword or court sword. Gentlemen continued to wear smallswords until the end of the 1700s, by which time duels were being fought with pistols (pp. 46-47).

**DUELING WITH RAPIERS**
An 18th-century drawing by English artist George Cruikshank for a novel called *The Miser's Daughter*. The duel is taking place in Tothill Fields in London, used as dueling grounds for several centuries.

*Knuckle guard*

**RAPIER, c. 1630**
In the 1500s, thrusting swords known as rapiers became popular with civilians. Because they had short grips and were impossible to hold with the whole hand, some rapiers had distinctive guards that protected the thumb and forefinger by partly covering the blade.

**"THE THREE MUSKETEERS"**
The famous historical novel by Alexandre Dumas takes place in France from 1625 to 1665. Wishing to become one of Louis XIII's guardsmen, D'Artagnan involves himself in duels with three famous swordsmen. The joint exploits of D'Artagnan and these three musketeers form the book's narrative.

*Guard, known as a pas d'ane, forming two loops that surround the sword's blade*

*Base of hilt resembling twigs or small branches*

*Counter-curved quillons (extend cross guards)*

## PARRYING WITH A DAGGER

The art of fighting with a rapier, known as fencing, was developed principally in France and Italy in the early 1600s. This engraving of a fencer practicing with a left-handed dagger was drawn by Jacques Callot.

## SMALLSWORD, c. 1740

In the early 17th century, the rapier began to be replaced by a lighter sword with a simpler hilt. Made in France, this smallsword would have been used both for dueling and as an item of everyday dress.

*Simple hilt with shell guard made of chiseled steel, partly gilt*

*Straight, double-edged blade - some mains gauches had prongs to catch an adversary's sword*

*As the grip is very short, the thumb extended onto the blade*

## BROADSWORD EXERCISES

From the 1600s, broadswords (pp. 44-45), swords with heavy, double-edged blades, were commonly used in European cavalry regiments. These three illustrations showing broadsword exercises come from an early 19th-century handkerchief.

*Cut 5*

*Cut 6*

## PARRYING DAGGER, c. 1650 *left*

A special dagger for parrying (blocking) an opponent's blow in dueling was misleadingly called a *main gauche* (French for "left hand"), even though it could be held in either hand.

## SIX BROADSWORD CUTS

A face on the handkerchief with the sword exercises (above) shows the directions of the six cuts that could be aimed at an opponent's head.

THE SIX CUTS

*Long, thin double-edged blade*

## FENCING MOVE, c. 1640

The swordsman on the right, using a rapier and parrying dagger, "passes" his adversary, and "disengages" under his dagger, thus killing him.

*Light, triangular - sectioned thrusting blade*

## A CELEBRATED FRENCH DUEL *right*

A 19th-century engraving depicts a duel, fought in Paris in 1578, that involved Henri III's favorite, Quèlus. The duelists' seconds also became involved, and at the end of the duel three men received fatal wounds, including Quèlus.

*Continued on next page*

### PRUSSIAN HUSSARS
The hussar (light cavalryman) on the right is carrying the type of saber that had become the main sword of European light cavalry by the beginning of the 19th century.

### SWORD CUTLER'S SHOP, c. 1755
In a Parisian sword cutler's shop, a customer is testing a new blade while workmen near the window are making sword hilts.

### BACKSWORD, c.1620
A backsword was a type of military sword used by European cavalry in the 17th century for both cutting and thrusting at an opponent in battle.

*Guard for protecting hand, similar to that of rapier*

Blade of 17th-century parrying dagger (p. 43)

Blade of 17th-century rapier (pp. 42-43)

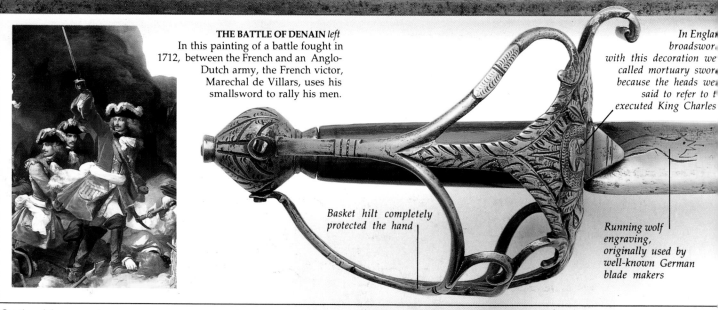

### THE BATTLE OF DENAIN *left*
In this painting of a battle fought in 1712, between the French and an Anglo-Dutch army, the French victor, Marechal de Villars, uses his smallsword to rally his men.

*In Engla... broadswor... with this decoration we... called mortuary swor... because the heads we... said to refer to t... executed King Charles*

*Basket hilt completely protected the hand*

*Running wolf engraving, originally used by well-known German blade makers*

Continued from previous page

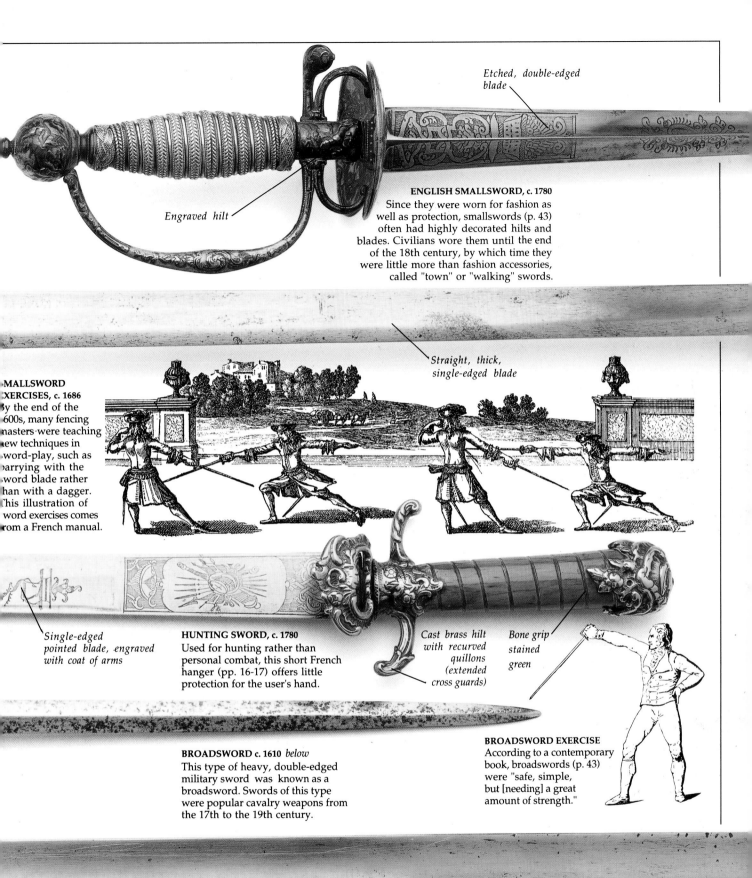

*Etched, double-edged blade*

*Engraved hilt*

### ENGLISH SMALLSWORD, c. 1780

Since they were worn for fashion as well as protection, smallswords (p. 43) often had highly decorated hilts and blades. Civilians wore them until the end of the 18th century, by which time they were little more than fashion accessories, called "town" or "walking" swords.

*Straight, thick, single-edged blade*

### SMALLSWORD EXERCISES, c. 1686

By the end of the 1600s, many fencing masters were teaching new techniques in sword-play, such as parrying with the sword blade rather than with a dagger. This illustration of sword exercises comes from a French manual.

*Single-edged pointed blade, engraved with coat of arms*

### HUNTING SWORD, c. 1780

Used for hunting rather than personal combat, this short French hanger (pp. 16-17) offers little protection for the user's hand.

*Cast brass hilt with recurved quillons (extended cross guards)*

*Bone grip stained green*

### BROADSWORD EXERCISE

According to a contemporary book, broadswords (p. 43) were "safe, simple, but [needing] a great amount of strength."

### BROADSWORD c. 1610 *below*

This type of heavy, double-edged military sword was known as a broadsword. Swords of this type were popular cavalry weapons from the 17th to the 19th century.

### 16TH-CENTURY HILTS

Far simpler than the rapier hilts designed to protect the hand in a duel is the hilt of the broadsword used by a *Landsknecht*, a German foot soldier, in the 1500s.

*A Landsknecht's broadsword and hilt*

# Dueling pistols

ALTHOUGH ILLEGAL, for centuries dueling was a popular way for "gentlemen" and army officers to settle their quarrels. By the late 18th century, when flintlock pistols were perfected, they had replaced swords (pp. 42-43) as the preferred method of fighting a duel. Gunsmiths began to make special dueling pistols in matched pairs, which they supplied fitted into a case with all the necessary accessories for both making the bullets and cleaning and loading the pistols. In order for dueling pistols to be as accurate as possible, the pistols were of the highest quality, with added refinements such as sights and special triggers. All dueling pistols were muzzle-loaders (pp. 38-39), and until about 1820-30 all used flintlock ignition.

*Spring-loaded trigger*

**SENSITIVE TRIGGER** *above*
Many dueling pistols had a special "hair" or "set" trigger, worked by an extra spring in the lock. These light triggers allowed the user to fire the pistol without disturbing his aim.

*The butt - rear part of stock*

*Wooden end for holding ramrod*

*The grip - part of stock where pistol is held*

**WOODEN STOCK** *right*
In all dueling pistols the wooden stock was carefully made so that the butt would fit comfortably in the duelist's hand. Some pistols had a squarer saw-handled butt to assist the grip.

**ALEKSANDR PUSHKIN**
Eminent men who took part in duels included the Duke of Wellington, a British general and statesman, and the French politician Georges Clemenceau. A famous victim was the great Russian writer Pushkin, killed in a duel with his wife's lover in 1837.

## Making a bullet

The lead ball or bullet was made at home by the firer, using a bullet mold provided with the pistol. Lead was melted over a fire and poured into the mold. After a few seconds the scissor-like mold was opened and the ball shaken out. Excess lead or "sprue" was cut off with the shears, which were part of the mold handles.

Black gunpowder

**LINEN PATCH**
To fit tightly in the barrel, the bullet was wrapped in a cloth or leather patch.

Lead bullets

*Nozzle forms a measure*

**RAMROD**
A wood or metal ramrod (kept in a recess below the barrel) was used to push the ball and patch down the bore. Many ramrods had special attachments for cleaning out the bore.

**BULLET MOLD**
Bullets were made by pouring melted lead into the hollow chamber of the bullet mold ( p. 57).

**POWDER FLASK**
Gunpowder was kept in a powder flask. Originally made of wood or horn (p. 39), by the 19th century most powder flasks were made of metal. When self-contained cartridges were introduced, powder flasks became obsolete.

*Metal end for ramming bullet down bore*

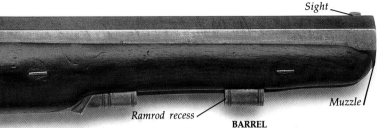

**AMERICAN ANTI-DUELING CARTOON, c. 1821** *left*
When this anti-dueling cartoon was published in Philadelphia, dueling was as popular in America as it was in France and England.

**AN AFFAIR OF HONOR, c. 1820**
Duels were called "affairs of honor." A gentleman who considered himself insulted by the behavior of another would challenge him to a duel. To refuse to be "called out" cast a bad slur on a gentleman's honor. The English artist Robert Cruikshank painted this duel at the height of the dueling era.

*Sight*

*Muzzle*

*Ramrod recess*

**BARREL**
Dueling pistols were muzzle-loaders (pp. 38-39). The outside of the barrel was usually octagonal in shape and fitted with sights.

**A PAIR OF ENGLISH DUELING PISTOLS, c. 1800 (lock of lower pistol shown separately)**

*Cock*

*Flint*

*Lock screw*

*Steel (frizzen)*

*Pan cover*

*Mainspring*

**LOCK** *left*
Screwed to the side of the stock, the lock was the mechanism that fired the pistol. When the trigger of a flintlock was pulled, the cock swung forward, making sparks by scraping the flint down the steel (or frizzen) and pushing open the pan cover. The sparks fell into the priming powder, which burned with a flash and set off the main powder charge in the barrel through the small touchhole.

**THE RULES OF DUELING**
In pistol duels combatants had to follow a strict set of rules. The exact rules of the fight were agreed between the two men and their "seconds" - friends who loaded the pistols and witnessed the duel. Usually, the two duelists stood an agreed number of paces apart, with their pistols pointing at the ground. At a given signal, such as the dropping of a handkerchief by one of the seconds, the duelists raised their pistols and fired.

## Cleaning a flintlock

1 Extract any unfired ball and powder from barrel using a special cleaning rod or tool attached to the ramrod.
2 Clean and oil empty barrel with cloth attached to ramrod or cleaning rod.
3 Brush away burned gunpowder in and around priming pan.
4 Oil lock.  5 Replace flint if worn out.

Oil can for oiling lock and barrel

A nonfatal duel, fought in France in 1893

*Spare leather*

**PAN BRUSH**
The priming pan needed frequent cleaning.

**FLINTS AND LEATHERS**
Leather was used to grip the flint in the jaws of the lock.

**TURNSCREW**
A turnscrew was used for removing the lock.

# Attack by highwaymen

IN THE LAWLESS days before guns were subject to licensing, many firearms were made or adapted for self-defense against armed robbers, either on the road or in the home. A gentleman on horseback could carry a pair of holster pistols on his saddle; when traveling by coach he could keep a small pistol in his coat pocket, or he or the coach's guard could carry a blunderbuss. The blunderbuss was well suited to close-range confrontations and was used to defend ships as well as travelers. Its wide muzzle helped scare an opponent and, if that didn't work, its charge of numerous lead balls gave its nervous owner a better chance of hitting the target. Blunderbusses were often fitted with spring bayonets for additional protection, and pistols butts could also be used as clubs. Inevitably, such weapons were equally suited to a robber's needs.

*Flintlock mechanism (some parts missing)*

**FOOTPADS ATTACKING A TRAVELER**
This 1813 cartoon by Thomas Rowlandson (p. 41) shows a traveler being held up by three "footpads" armed with pocket pistols.

**FLINTLOCK BLUNDERBUSS**
Blunderbusses fired a number o small shot for close-range effect This late 18th-century blunderbus has a spring-loaded bayonet - or releasing the catch the bayonet woul flip forward and lock in position

*Ramrod*

*Flintlock mechanism of box-lock type*

*Two brass barrels side by side*

**POCKET PISTOL**
With a double-barrele pistol, both barrels were fired by the same lock. The iron slider on the boxlike frame selected which barrel was connected with the flash pan. This particular pocket pisto was made in London, c. 1785

*Silver butt cap*

Partially opened
spring bayonet

Bayonet spring
and lock

Bayonet
catch

Brass barrel

Ramrod

**DICK TURPIN** *left*
During the 1730s Dick Turpin, the legendary highwayman, was the most wanted man in England. Here Turpin is shown improbably firing two pistols in opposite directions, while jumping a tollgate on his famous horse, Black Bess.

**TRICORN HAT**
A three-cornered or tricorn hat would have been worn by the more respectable 18th-century highwayman.

**ROBERT MACAIRE**
During the 18th century celebrated highwaymen soon became folk heroes. Here, a notorious robber called Robert Macaire is being portrayed by an actor named Mr. Hicks.

**HOLSTER PISTOL**
The butt cap of this early 18th-century holster pistol allowed the pistol to be reversed and used as a club once the single shot had been fired.

Brass mounted

Butt cap

**AN ATTACK BY HIGHWAYMEN**
In 1750 two highwaymen robbed Lord Eglinton, who was riding in his carriage near London. On this occasion the blunderbuss his lordship is holding proved useless.

# Bizarre hand weapons

THROUGHOUT recorded history extraordinary and seemingly impractical weapons have been made alongside conventional swords, guns, and bows and arrows. The unusual weapons shown on these pages prove that many local and tribal weapons were just as ingenious and deadly as the specialist weapons devised for close-range attack and defense, or the strange-looking combination pistols made by gunsmiths for their rich customers.

**ITALIAN GUNNER'S STILETTO** *below*
The engraving on the blade of this 18th-century dagger is a numbered scale for artillery commanders to calculate the bore size of cannons.

*Engraved blade*

**"CROW'S FEET"** c. 19th century *left*
First used in the 4th century B.C., caltrops or "crow's feet" are made of four or more sharp iron spikes. They were thrown in front of horse's hooves or infantrymen's feet.

*Single-edged curved blade*

**THE LAST ARMOR** *below*
In the 1700s and 1800s the only piece of armor regularly worn by European or American armies was the gorget (p. 26), worn as a mark of rank for officers rather than for defense. Today gorgets are still used with full dress in some countries. This particular gorget (below) belonged to an officer of the marines in the British navy, c. 1800.

*Dagger blade*

*Gorget*

*Trigger*

*Barrel concealed in brass handle*

*Weapon fired when turned muzzle plugs were removed*

**CUTLERY PISTOLS** *right*
Among the most impractical flintlock firearms ever devised must be this companion knife and fork, made in Germany about 1740.

**GURKHA KNIFE** *right*
The *kukri* is the national knife and principal weapon of the Gurkhas of Nepal. Although the *kukri* is useful for cutting through jungle, its heavy, curved blade also makes it a deadly fighting weapon.

**INDIAN MACE** *right*
This all-steel mace was made in India in the 19th century. The owner would have used the mace to lean on while he was sitting down but could have quickly clubbed any possible enemy with the metal "hand."

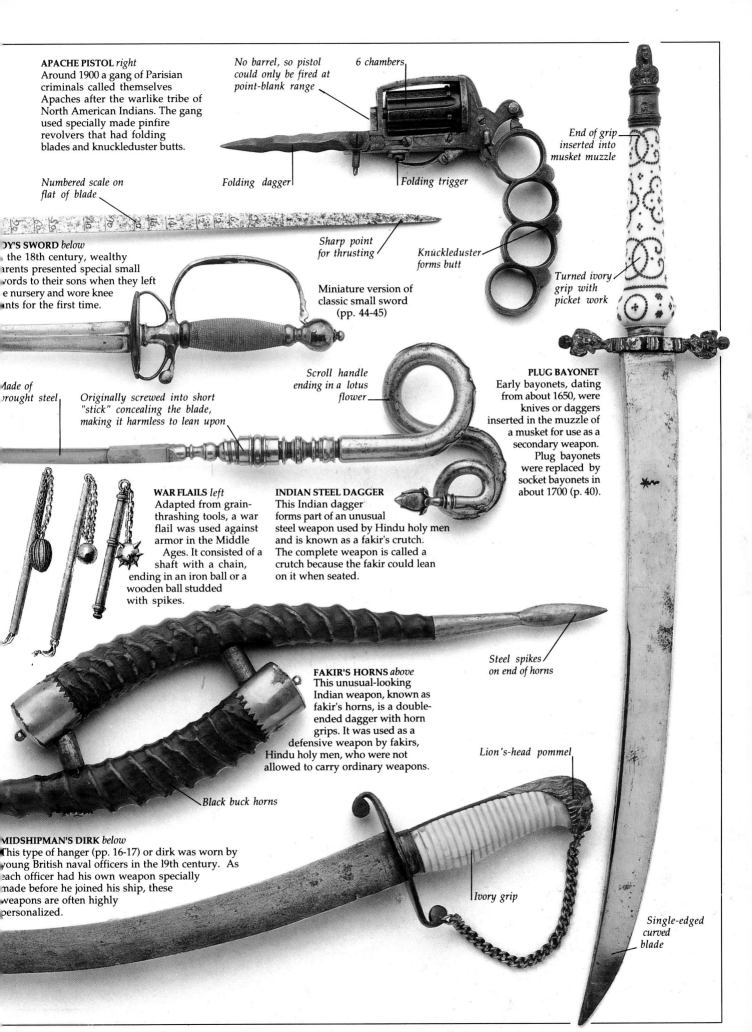

**APACHE PISTOL** *right*
Around 1900 a gang of Parisian criminals called themselves Apaches after the warlike tribe of North American Indians. The gang used specially made pinfire revolvers that had folding blades and knuckleduster butts.

*No barrel, so pistol could only be fired at point-blank range*

*6 chambers*

*Folding dagger*

*Folding trigger*

*End of grip inserted into musket muzzle*

*Numbered scale on flat of blade*

*Sharp point for thrusting*

*Knuckleduster forms butt*

*Turned ivory grip with picket work*

**OY'S SWORD** *below*
the 18th century, wealthy arents presented special small words to their sons when they left e nursery and wore knee nts for the first time.

*Miniature version of classic small sword (pp. 44-45)*

*Made of rought steel*

*Originally screwed into short "stick" concealing the blade, making it harmless to lean upon*

*Scroll handle ending in a lotus flower*

**PLUG BAYONET**
Early bayonets, dating from about 1650, were knives or daggers inserted in the muzzle of a musket for use as a secondary weapon. Plug bayonets were replaced by socket bayonets in about 1700 (p. 40).

**WAR FLAILS** *left*
Adapted from grain-thrashing tools, a war flail was used against armor in the Middle Ages. It consisted of a shaft with a chain, ending in an iron ball or a wooden ball studded with spikes.

**INDIAN STEEL DAGGER**
This Indian dagger forms part of an unusual steel weapon used by Hindu holy men and is known as a fakir's crutch. The complete weapon is called a crutch because the fakir could lean on it when seated.

*Steel spikes on end of horns*

**FAKIR'S HORNS** *above*
This unusual-looking Indian weapon, known as fakir's horns, is a double-ended dagger with horn grips. It was used as a defensive weapon by fakirs, Hindu holy men, who were not allowed to carry ordinary weapons.

*Lion's-head pommel*

*Black buck horns*

**MIDSHIPMAN'S DIRK** *below*
This type of hanger (pp. 16-17) or dirk was worn by young British naval officers in the l9th century. As each officer had his own weapon specially made before he joined his ship, these weapons are often highly personalized.

*Ivory grip*

*Single-edged curved blade*

# Grenadiers and cavalry

**FRENCH GRENADIER**
Despite his title, the main weapon of this soldier in the French Light Infantry was his flintlock musket.

**GRENADIER'S POUCH AND BELT**
An 18th-century English grenadier's pouch decorated with a one-legged grenadier. Grenadiers of this period wore special pointed caps to enable them to throw grenades overarm.

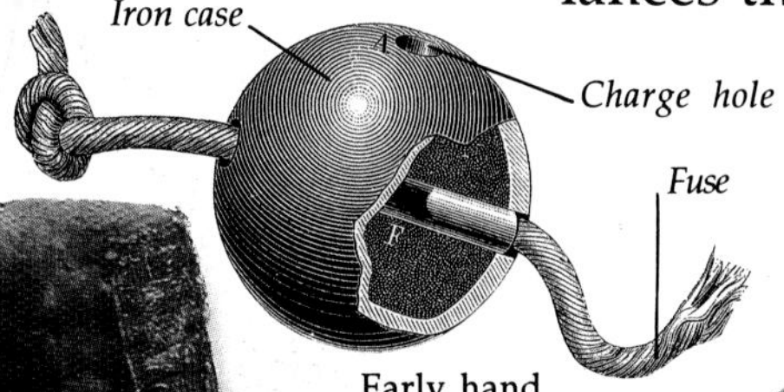

*Brass match case*

*Brush for removing excess gunpowder*

BY THE TIME Napoleon Bonaparte was conquering most of Europe at the beginning of the 1800s, flintlock firearms - muskets, carbines, and pistols - had become the chief weapons of armies in both Europe and North America (pp. 40-41). Among the specialist flintlocks were grenade launchers - weapons for destroying defensive works such as doorways and barricades. Originally grenades were used by specially trained troops called grenadiers. But by the 19th century most so-called grenadiers were ordinary infantry corps who used flintlock muskets rather than grenades. In the Napoleonic Wars (1796-1815) muskets proved such unbeatable weapons that they often destroyed the effectiveness of mounted troops, who relied more on swords and lances than firearms.

*Iron case*

*Charge hole*

*Fuse*

Early hand grenade

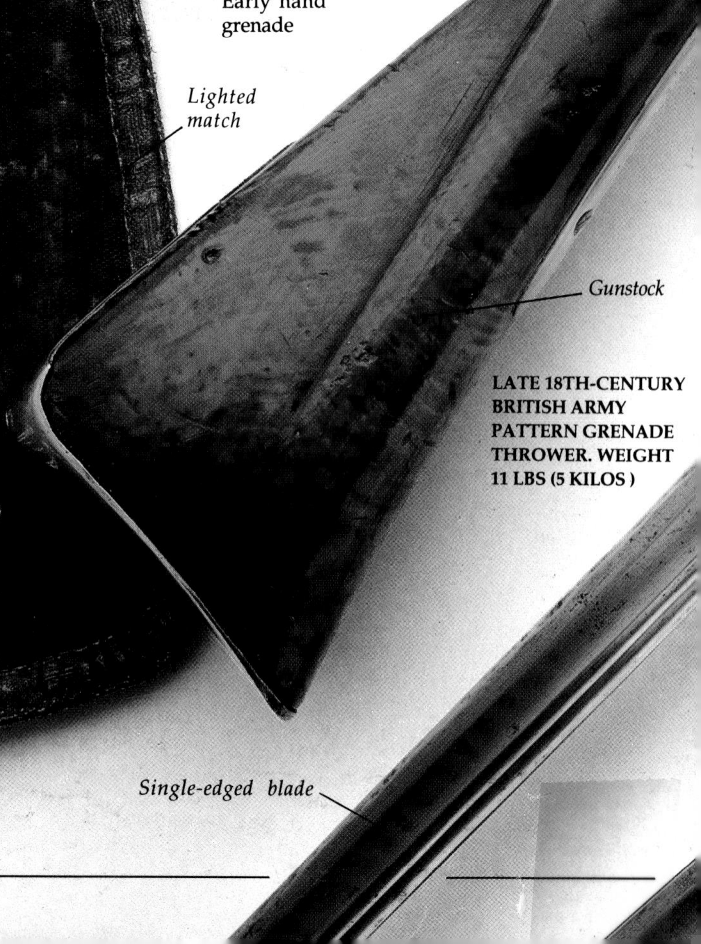

*Velvet pouch*

*Grenade*

*Grenade pouch*

*Lighted match*

*Gunstock*

**LATE 18TH-CENTURY BRITISH ARMY PATTERN GRENADE THROWER. WEIGHT 11 LBS (5 KILOS)**

I LOVE AND HONOUR

*Live grenade*

*Buff leather belt*

*Single-edged blade*

## SOLDIER LIGHTING GRENADE *left*

By the late 1600s small bombs known as hand grenades were commonly used in European battles. Early grenades were hollow iron balls filled with black gunpowder. Holes were bored through the wall of the grenade (below left) and threaded with a short fuse.

## GRENADE LAUNCHER

This fearsome weapon, designed to increase the range of grenades, first appeared in the l6th century. Any mistake in lighting the grenade fuse was liable to cause fatal injuries to the grenadier and anybody nearby.

*16 ins (40 cm) long barrel*

## CAVALRY CHARGE

At the Battle of Waterloo in 1815 a series of classic encounters took place as the French light cavalry charged the British infantry squares. While one line of the square fired a volley, another line reloaded. In this battle the inability of the French cavalry to break through these squares proved decisive.

*Fleur-de-lis*

## CAVALRY SWORD

Late 18th-century French saber with a brass hilt decorated with a fleur-de-lis, the royal emblem of France. The sword has a single-edged, straight blade.

## BRITISH OFFICER'S SHAKO, EARLY 19TH CENTURY

*Basket hilt protects the entire hand*

*Engraving reads* Pro Deo fide et Patria - "For God, Faith and Country"

Napoleon Bonaparte in l812

## CUIRASSIER'S SWORD

French saber with the gilded brass hilt and slightly curved blade of the type used by cuirassier or heavy cavalry regiments in Napoleon's army.

## OFFICER'S SHAKO

In the l800s shakos, stiff peaked caps, were worn in many armies (also top of opposite page).

# Keeping law and order

Sɪɴᴄᴇ ᴛʜᴇ ᴡᴏʀᴅ "ᴘᴏʟɪᴄᴇ" ᴍᴇᴀɴs different types of forces in different countries - civilian and military, uniformed and plain-clothed - the batons, rattles, and other law-enforcement equipment shown on these pages are best described as weapons for combating crime and keeping public order. All of them were in use during the 19th century, and when it is considered how much violent crime and civilian unrest took place during the 1800s, these weapons seem hardly sufficent. Of course, more powerful weapons were issued to some police forces of necessity - by the late 19th century the Berlin police were armed with swords, pistols, and brass knuckles, and the police in New York and Boston first used firearms during the 1850s. But in most European and American towns the increasing respect felt for the ordinary civilian law-enforcement officer was due in part to his being so lightly armed.

**LONDON POLICEMAN**
A late 19th-century policeman goes on night patrol with just a truncheon and a lamp.

**POLICE SWORD** *below*
Short swords were issued to 19th-century police forces and to prison guards. In Britain they were not standard equipment, but were kept in police stations or prisons, for use in riots or other emergencies.

*Leather hilt with brass mounts*

*Brass guard and pommel*

*Brass mount*

*Originally had a wooden clapper that made a penetrating sound*

*Lead weights gave extra weight when swung*

**POLICE RATTLES**
Lead weights in a rattle (above) made it a useful weapon as well as giving it extra weight when it was swung. Rattles with clappers (right) made an especially loud noise.

**PICTUREBOOK POLICEMAN**
The fact that images of 19th-century policemen were often used to frighten children into behaving properly is well illustrated by this picture of a policeman in a child's gift book dating from 1867.

**POLICE WHISTLE** *right*
Whistles were adopted in many police forces during the 19th century when it was found that they could be heard over far greater distances than the sound from a rattle.

*Buckle for securing at the back of neck*

**LEATHER COLLAR**
In some early police forces officers wore leather collars called stocks to protect them from being garroted - strangled with a cord. Stocks were both hot and restrictive to wear.

*Stock is 4 ins (10 cms) wide*

*Twin handles*

*Outer tin shell*

*Ground-glass magnifying lens*

**BULLSEYE LANTERN**
The standard British police lamp in the 19th century, the bullseye lantern hooked onto the belt the policeman wore over his greatcoat.

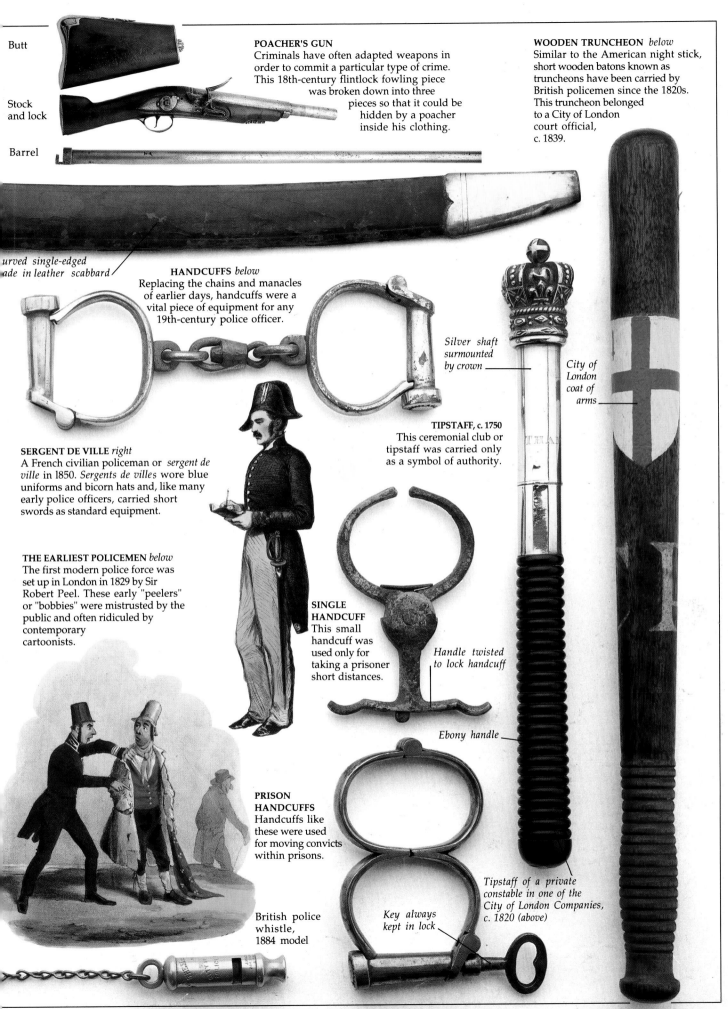

**POACHER'S GUN**
Criminals have often adapted weapons in order to commit a particular type of crime. This 18th-century flintlock fowling piece was broken down into three pieces so that it could be hidden by a poacher inside his clothing.

Butt

Stock and lock

Barrel

**WOODEN TRUNCHEON** *below*
Similar to the American night stick, short wooden batons known as truncheons have been carried by British policemen since the 1820s. This truncheon belonged to a City of London court official, c. 1839.

urved single-edged
ade in leather scabbard

**HANDCUFFS** *below*
Replacing the chains and manacles of earlier days, handcuffs were a vital piece of equipment for any 19th-century police officer.

*Silver shaft surmounted by crown*

*City of London coat of arms*

**SERGENT DE VILLE** *right*
A French civilian policeman or *sergent de ville* in 1850. *Sergents de villes* wore blue uniforms and bicorn hats and, like many early police officers, carried short swords as standard equipment.

**TIPSTAFF, c. 1750**
This ceremonial club or tipstaff was carried only as a symbol of authority.

**THE EARLIEST POLICEMEN** *below*
The first modern police force was set up in London in 1829 by Sir Robert Peel. These early "peelers" or "bobbies" were mistrusted by the public and often ridiculed by contemporary cartoonists.

**SINGLE HANDCUFF**
This small handcuff was used only for taking a prisoner short distances.

*Handle twisted to lock handcuff*

*Ebony handle*

**PRISON HANDCUFFS**
Handcuffs like these were used for moving convicts within prisons.

British police whistle, 1884 model

*Tipstaff of a private constable in one of the City of London Companies, c. 1820 (above)*

*Key always kept in lock*

# The percussion revolver

PERCUSSION IGNITION was an important development in the history of firearms. In the early 19th century it offered instant ignition and greatly improved resistance to wet weather. In its most common form a thimble-cap containing an explosive compound was placed on a steel nipple. When struck by the weapon's hammer the cap exploded, sending a jet of flame through the nipple into the powder charge. Early percussion guns were still muzzleloaders (pp. 38-39), with the cap separate from the powder and ball. Later, the cap was incorporated in the base of a self-contained metallic cartridge, with the powder and ball. The metal case sealed in the explosive gases, allowing efficient breech-loading designs that are still in world-wide use today.

**SHERLOCK HOLMES**
An actor portraying the most famous detective in literature, Sherlock Holmes, is shown holding a smoking percussion pistol.

**PERCUSSION REVOLVER**
A percussion revolver, c.1855, made by the English gunmaker William Tranter. This self-cocking double-action design could be used with one hand. Pulling the lower trigger turned the cylinder and cocked the hammer; pulling the upper trigger fired the shot.

Back sight

Five-shot revolving cylinder

Hammer or cock

Nipple

Button for opening gun at axis

Linen tape to close bag

Upper trigger

Linen bag

Lower trigger

**INDIAN MUTINY, 1857** *below*
In the kind of hand-to-hand fighting that took place in the Indian Mutiny, British officers preferred self-cocking revolvers (like the Tranter), for rapid firing.

**BAG OF CARTRIDGES**
To load the revolver, the copper cover was removed from the paper sachet of powder attached to the bullet, and the cartridge was loaded into the front of the revolver cylinder. The revolver would have been equipped with a detachable rammer.

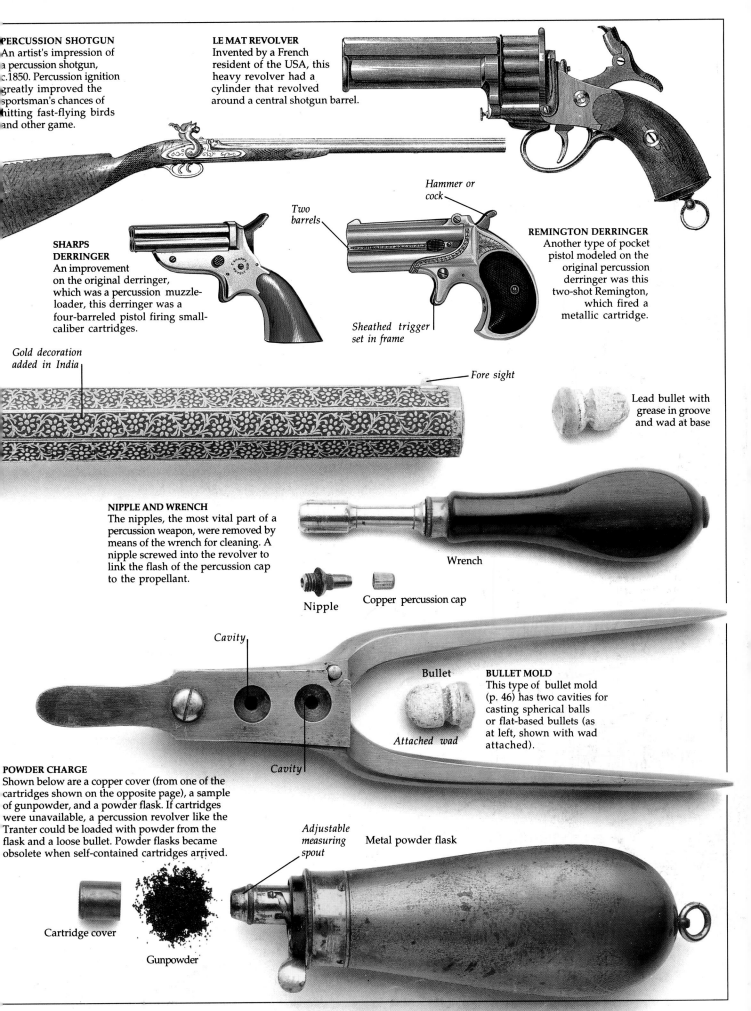

**PERCUSSION SHOTGUN**
An artist's impression of a percussion shotgun, c.1850. Percussion ignition greatly improved the sportsman's chances of hitting fast-flying birds and other game.

**LE MAT REVOLVER**
Invented by a French resident of the USA, this heavy revolver had a cylinder that revolved around a central shotgun barrel.

*Hammer or cock*

*Two barrels*

**SHARPS DERRINGER**
An improvement on the original derringer, which was a percussion muzzle-loader, this derringer was a four-barreled pistol firing small-caliber cartridges.

**REMINGTON DERRINGER**
Another type of pocket pistol modeled on the original percussion derringer was this two-shot Remington, which fired a metallic cartridge.

*Sheathed trigger set in frame*

*Gold decoration added in India*

*Fore sight*

Lead bullet with grease in groove and wad at base

**NIPPLE AND WRENCH**
The nipples, the most vital part of a percussion weapon, were removed by means of the wrench for cleaning. A nipple screwed into the revolver to link the flash of the percussion cap to the propellant.

Wrench

Nipple

Copper percussion cap

*Cavity*

**Bullet**

**BULLET MOLD**
This type of bullet mold (p. 46) has two cavities for casting spherical balls or flat-based bullets (as at left, shown with wad attached).

*Attached wad*

*Cavity*

**POWDER CHARGE**
Shown below are a copper cover (from one of the cartridges shown on the opposite page), a sample of gunpowder, and a powder flask. If cartridges were unavailable, a percussion revolver like the Tranter could be loaded with powder from the flask and a loose bullet. Powder flasks became obsolete when self-contained cartridges arrived.

*Adjustable measuring spout*

Metal powder flask

Cartridge cover

Gunpowder

# Pistols

A PISTOL IS SIMPLY a short-barreled firearm designed to be used with one hand - a convenient weapon to carry but needing much practice to fire accurately. During the 19th century a great number of pistols were designed for both military and civilian use. Some could fire only a single shot but others - called revolvers - could fire several shots in a row before they needed reloading.

**OPEN CYLINDER**
The open cylinder of a Colt revolver, shown at the moment when the empty cartridge cases are ejected, before reloading.

*One of three bands for holding barrel in stock*

**COSSACK PISTOL**
A pistol from the Caucasus in southern Russia with a miquelet lock - a type of flintlock used mainly in Spain and the Middle East. Cossack warriors used similar pistols in the 18th and 19th century.

**"BUNTLINE SPECIAL" REVOLVER** *above*
This long-barreled version of the Colt Peacemaker (p. 61) was made famous by the 19th-century American writer Ned Buntline, author of over 400 action novels.

*Hammer*

**TRANSITIONAL REVOLVER** *above*
Representing the "transition" between the pepperbox and the true revolver, this weapon was cheap and popular during the 1850s.

**ASSASSIN'S PISTOL** *below*
This unusual revolver, known as a palm pistol or "lemon squeezer," was held almost hidden in the hand and fired by a squeezing action. One was used to assassinate President William McKinley in 1901.

*7-shot cylinder*

*Barrel*

*Hammer*

*Six barrels*

*Trigger rotates the barrel and fires the shot*

**PEPPERBOX REVOLVER**
The pepperbox was an early form of revolver, with a cluster of barrels, the muzzles of which resembled holes in a pepperpot. Pepperboxes were popular between 1830 and 1860, despite their unreliability.

Bullet mold for
combination pistol

Folding dagger
blade

Pistol barrel

**COMBINATION PISTOL**
A popular weapon of the 1840s and
'50s was the combined pistol and
pocketknife. This example
includes a pistol, two knife
blades, a ramrod, and
space in the grip for
ammunition.

Folding pocket-
knife blade

Folding
trigger

Hollow grip
for ammunition and
bullet mold

Decorative gilt
and Niello work

Ramrod

Special 12 in (305 mm) barrel

**POCKET OR MUFF PISTOL**
This percussion pistol, c. 1850, was kept in a
man's pocket or a lady's muff. Its trigger
folded into the pistol when not in use.

A .36 caliber
cartridge for the
Colt Police Revolver

**COLT POLICE
REVOLVER** *above*
Among the many types of pistol
produced by Colt from the 1830s
onwards was the Model 1862 Police
Revolver, a gun firing five shots.

Lanyard ring for
cord attaching
pistol around
the neck or
shoulder

Ejector rod to
knock out empty
cartridge cases

**PINFIRE CARTRIDGE**
The pistol's hammer
struck the brass pin,
which set off a detonator
inside the cartridge.

Two barrels

**FRENCH PINFIRE REVOLVER**
Pinfire weapons were among the
first to use a self-contained cartridge
in which bullet, powder, and cap
were all held in a brass case. The
cartridge could be loaded quickly
from the breech end, and its
case kept the explosion from leaking
back toward the firer's hand. This
revolver dates from about 1855.

**"OVER-AND-UNDER" PISTOL**
This English pocket pistol,
c. 1820, has two barrels, one above the
other. Each has its own flintlock
mechanism, but a clever design
allows both barrels to be fired by
just one trigger.

Single trigger

# Guns that won the West

T HE WESTWARD EXPANSION of the United States in the 19th century coincided with a period of rapid development in firearms, and the new arms were used alike by settlers, cowboys, the army, Indians, and outlaws. The most popular weapons were revolvers such as those made by Samuel Colt, and repeating rifles such as the Winchester, which were light enough for use as a carbine on horseback and more accurate than a revolver at longer ranges on the open plains.

Buffalo Bill, holding a Winchester '73, with the Sioux chief Sitting Bull

Lever

Iron butt plate

Lever incorporated with trigger guard pushed forward and back between shots

Spare cartridge

Walnut stock

Belt loop

**GUNBELT AND HOLSTER**
This much-used 19th-century gunbelt and holster is similar to the one worn by the US cavalry officer in campaign dress (inset), drawn by artist Frederic Remington (1861-1909). Note the spare cartridges in the belt loops.

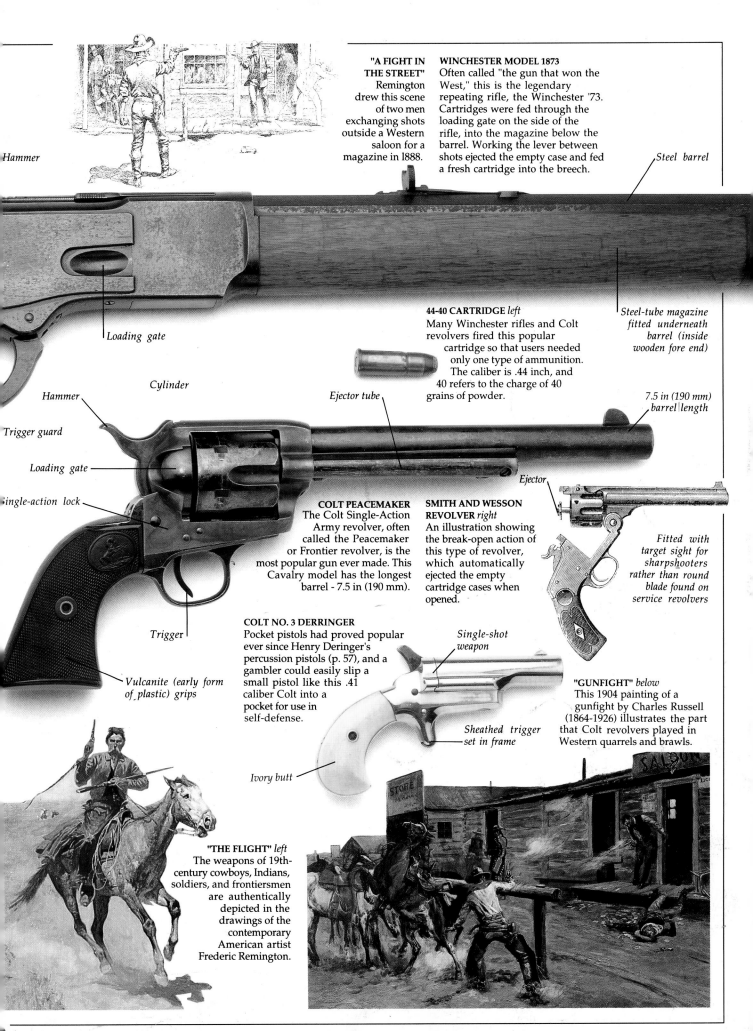

**Hammer**

**"A FIGHT IN THE STREET"**
Remington drew this scene of two men exchanging shots outside a Western saloon for a magazine in 1888.

**WINCHESTER MODEL 1873**
Often called "the gun that won the West," this is the legendary repeating rifle, the Winchester '73. Cartridges were fed through the loading gate on the side of the rifle, into the magazine below the barrel. Working the lever between shots ejected the empty case and fed a fresh cartridge into the breech.

*Steel barrel*

**44-40 CARTRIDGE** *left*
Many Winchester rifles and Colt revolvers fired this popular cartridge so that users needed only one type of ammunition. The caliber is .44 inch, and 40 refers to the charge of 40 grains of powder.

*Steel-tube magazine fitted underneath barrel (inside wooden fore end)*

*Loading gate*

*Cylinder*

*Ejector tube*

*7.5 in (190 mm) barrel length*

**Hammer**

**Trigger guard**

**Loading gate**

**Single-action lock**

*Ejector*

**COLT PEACEMAKER**
The Colt Single-Action Army revolver, often called the Peacemaker or Frontier revolver, is the most popular gun ever made. This Cavalry model has the longest barrel - 7.5 in (190 mm).

**SMITH AND WESSON REVOLVER** *right*
An illustration showing the break-open action of this type of revolver, which automatically ejected the empty cartridge cases when opened.

*Fitted with target sight for sharpshooters rather than round blade found on service revolvers*

**Trigger**

*Vulcanite (early form of plastic) grips*

**COLT NO. 3 DERRINGER**
Pocket pistols had proved popular ever since Henry Deringer's percussion pistols (p. 57), and a gambler could easily slip a small pistol like this .41 caliber Colt into a pocket for use in self-defense.

*Single-shot weapon*

*Sheathed trigger set in frame*

*Ivory butt*

**"GUNFIGHT"** *below*
This 1904 painting of a gunfight by Charles Russell (1864-1926) illustrates the part that Colt revolvers played in Western quarrels and brawls.

**"THE FLIGHT"** *left*
The weapons of 19th-century cowboys, Indians, soldiers, and frontiersmen are authentically depicted in the drawings of the contemporary American artist Frederic Remington.

# North American Indians

WRONGLY CALLED *Indios* by Christopher Columbus, the native inhabitants of North America once totaled between one and two million people. However, between 1492 and 1900 the Indian tribes were nearly wiped out, as European settlers forced their own way of life on the woodlands and prairies. After initial peaceful contacts with white traders, the tribes who fought hardest to prevent the white man's takeover of their lands in the 1800s were those who lived on the Great Plains and in the Southwest. The Plains Indians lived in the central grasslands, where the more nomadic (roaming) tribes among them hunted the herds of buffalo that crossed the prairies. Other Indian tribes such as the Apaches, fierce warriors from the Southwest, tended to live in one place. Before they obtained European rifles, the tribes in both these areas used basically the same weapons - bows and arrows (p. 9), knives (pp. 22-23), clubs, and the weapon most strongly associated with the North American Indian, the tomahawk.

A typical mask worn by Indians during religious ceremonies

*Finely honed stone blade*

**STONE-BLADED KNIFE**
All Indians owned knives. This one was made in 1900 by a Hupa Indian from California. By 1900, many Indians had steel-bladed knives.

**HIAWATHA**
An Ojibwa Indian, Hiawatha was the hero of a long narrative poem written in 1855 by Henry Longfellow. In it, Hiawatha becomes leader of his people and teaches peace with the white man.

*Feather decoration*

*Cloth strips bound with buckskin*

*Quiver made of buckskin*

*Bow made of ash*

**QUIVER**

**WAR BOW, c. 1850**
Until they began to acquire rifles in the 1850s and '60s, Plains Indians' bows were their most important weapons, used for both hunting and warfare. Made of ash, this bow belonged to an Omaha warrior.

*Nock or groove for attachment of bowstring*

**BOW CASE**

**BOW CASE AND QUIVER**
For easier carrying on horseback, a Plains Indian had a combined quiver and bow case. Bow accessories were usually made of buckskin.

**BUFFALO HUNTING**
Painter George Catlin spent six years among the Plains Indians, recording their way of life in the early 1800s. In this painting, Indians are hunting buffalo.

**TOMAHAWK PIPE, c. 1890**
This tomahawk pipe was supposedly made by the great Apache chief Geronimo during his exile in Florida.

*Tomahawk blade*

**EAGLE FEATHER HEADDRESS** *left*
In this 1907 photograph, the eagle feather headdress, worn by Iron Plume, a Plains Indian chieftain, was seen only at ceremonies and celebrations.

*Bowstring made of two buffalo sinews twisted together*

**ARROWS** *below*
A Plains Indian's arrowheads would have been made from buffalo bones. In other regions, Indians made stone arrowheads.

*Feathered flights*

*Wooden shafts frequently painted with symbolic designs*

*Iron tobacco bowl*

*Buckskin grip*

An Indian with a war club fights another wielding a tomahawk

*Engraving on blade, c. 1800, shows Indian threatening a European*

*Iron tobacco bowl*

*Hollow handle*

**APACHE TOMAHAWK PIPE**
Before European traders supplied the Indians with iron, they made their tomahawk heads with stone. The type of tomahawk that combined an axe blade with a tobacco bowl was usually made by Europeans for trading with the Indians.

63

# Index

# Acknowledgments

**Picture credits**
t=top b=bottom l=left r=right c=centre

Reproduced by Courtesy of the Trustees of the British Museum: 14bm
E.T. Archives: 8b
Giraudon: 43tl
Goteborg Museum of Art: 39m
India Office Library (British Library): 33t
John Freeman London: 16br; 18m, tr; 19mr; 21tr; 26b; 28mr, bl; 30tm; 31; 39t; 40m; 42b; 44tl; 52t; 53b; 54t; 62tl, tr, m
H.Josse, Paris: 44b
Mansell Collection: 11m; 42m
Mary Evans Picture Library: 6b; 7bl; 8m; 9b; 12t, br; 13t, b; 14bl; 16bl, t; 17tr, tr; 19t; 20t, m, b; 22t, m; 23m; 24b; 25m, b; 26tl, tr; 27b; 28bm; 29bl, br; 30m, tl, tr; 34tl; 35t; 36m; 38m, b; 39b; 40tl; 44tr;

47tr, b;48m; 49m, b; 51m; 52tr, m; 54t, b; 55m, b; 56t; 57tl, tr; 58tl, tr, b; 60b; 61m,t
Sheridan Photo Library: 7br
Michael Holford: 12bl; 15t, m, b; 32b; 36-37t; 63t
National Army Museum: 53t
Peter Newark's Western Americana and Historical Pictures: 14br; 29m; 37m; 41b; 46t; 47tl; 56b; 60t; 61br; 63b
Robert Hunt Library: 21m
Ronald Sheridan: 7br
Tower of London Royal Armouries: 25t
Visual Arts Library: 43tr, m; 61bl

Illustrations on p. 6 by Coral Mula.

**Dorling Kindersley would like to thank:**
City of London Police: pp. 54-55; also Police Constable Ray Hayter for his assistance.
Pitt Rivers Museum, University of Oxford, Oxford ; pp. 4-5, 22-23, 32-33, 36-37; also John Todd for his assistance.
Ermine Street Guard; pp. 1,12-13; also Nicholas Fuentes for his assistance.
Museum of London: pp. 6-7, 12bl, 10-11, 14-15; also Nick Merriman, Peter Stott and Gavin Morgan for their assistance.
Museum of Mankind, British Museum: pp. 8-9, 62-63.
National Army Museum: pp. 56-57;

also Stephen Bull for his assistance.
Warwick Castle, Warwick: pp. 16-17, 24-25, 26-27, 28-29, 30-31, 38-39, 40-41, 42-43, 44-45, 48-49,52-53, 55t; also F.H.P. Barker for his assistance.
Robin Wigington, Arbour Antiques, Ltd., Stratford-upon-Avon: pp. 2-3, 18-19, 20-21, 34-35, 38b, 50-51, 58-59, 60-61.
Anne-Marie Bulat for her work on the initial stages of the book.
Martyn Foote for design assistance.
Fred Ford and Mike Pilley of Radius Graphics, and Ray Owen and Nick Madren for artwork.
Jonathan Buckley for his assistance on the photographic sessions.